The Children's War

The Children's War

Britain, 1914–1918

Rosie Kennedy
Visiting Tutor, Goldsmiths College, University of London

palgrave
macmillan

First published 2014 by
PALGRAVE MACMILLAN

Palgrave Macmillan in the UK is an imprint of Macmillan Publishers Limited,
registered in England, company number 785998, of Houndmills, Basingstoke,
Hampshire RG21 6XS.

Palgrave Macmillan in the US is a division of St Martin's Press LLC,
175 Fifth Avenue, New York, NY 10010.

Palgrave Macmillan is the global academic imprint of the above companies
and has companies and representatives throughout the world.

Palgrave® and Macmillan® are registered trademarks in the United States,
the United Kingdom, Europe and other countries.

ISBN 978–0–230–22175–8

This book is printed on paper suitable for recycling and made from fully
managed and sustained forest sources. Logging, pulping and manufacturing
processes are expected to conform to the environmental regulations of the
country of origin.

A catalogue record for this book is available from the British Library.

A catalog record for this book is available from the Library of Congress.

*For my Dad whose memories of a Second World War childhood
inspired this project
And for my Mum with all my love*

Contents

Illustrations

Acknowledgements

During the course of preparing this book for publication I have had the pleasure of corresponding with the families of some of the soldiers and children who wrote to each other during the First World War. I would like to thank the following people for allowing me to use their family papers in this book: Ann Proctor for the papers of A.C. Stanton; Dick Butling for the papers of G. and E. Butling; Ray Oakley for the papers of W. Vernon; Dorothy Griffiths for the papers of J. Hancock; Sheila Juma for the papers of H. Bearer; Eileen Buckeridge for the papers of E.G. Buckeridge; Alida Robinson for the papers of I. Finn; Elspeth Grisenthwaite for the papers of J.B. Foulis; Yvonne Long for the papers of F.H. Gautier; Bertha Burgess for the papers of H.N. Hignett; Gyllian Pearson for the papers of E. Hopkinson; Heather MacDonald for the papers of D. Tickner and Annette Kuhn for the memoirs of her mother Minnie Cowley.

Every effort has been made to trace the copyright holders for the papers of R.P. Harker and E.I. Williams, and the author and the Imperial War Museum would be grateful for any information that might help to trace those whose identities or addresses are not currently known.

The author and publishers would also be very grateful for any information relating to the current copyright holders of the following memoirs held in the Burnett Working Class Autobiographical Archive at Brunel University:

Armitage, J.H. 'The Twenty Three Years. Or the Late Way of Life and of Living.'
Betterton, K. ' "White Pinnies, Black Aprons....".'
Jacobs, A.P. 'Just Take a Look at These.'
Keen, M. 'Childhood Memories 1903–1921.'

Additional material is reproduced with kind permission of:

Girl Guiding UK
The Trustees of the Scout Association
City of London Metropolitan Archives
The British Library

The Imperial War Museum
The Old Toy Soldier Newsletter

Since beginning this book I have become a mother twice over. Trying to write while at home with two small children is not easy, and I would like to thank my editors at Palgrave for their patience and understanding. In the absence of work colleagues, their anonymous readers provided a much-needed fresh perspective, and I would like to thank them for their comments and advice.

I will also always be grateful to my supervisor, Professor Sally Alexander, for her help and expert guidance. Sally has become the critic in my head and I now find it impossible to write anything without first imagining what she would say about it.

This book would never have been finished without the love, support and encouragement of my family. I would especially like to thank my husband Ben for sharing the juggling act that is family life, and for making sure this book had its turn as a priority. Finally, thank you to Grace and Annie for reminding me what it is like to be a child and for teaching me what it means to be a parent, and for trying to understand when Mummy sometimes wants to do some work.

1
Introduction

Beatrice Curtis Brown believes that the outbreak of the First World War marked a turning point in her life, a moment when she ceased to be a child and recognised for the first time the significance of the outside world. She writes:

> Infancy, I suppose, stopped with the war at least, home, London, became something different with the war. Though I was thirteen when it broke out, my memory of places, what we did and how we felt, is up to that time, tuned to the same key. Then some discordancy creeps in: one's world was no longer apart and enclosed by its own walls. The day before war broke out is the first day I remember walking about London, as apart from Hampstead, streets. That is, it was the first time that I was conscious of being there in the middle of the city.[1]

The historian A.L. Rowse, whose autobiography *A Cornish Childhood* was published in 1942, also believes that the start of the war was the point at which he realised there was a world outside his own:

> It had a strange significance for me, which is not wholly explicable. It was a symbolic day. For the first time I became aware of the outer world, a world beyond the village and the town. I was ten years old.[2]

For both these writers the First World War was a dividing line in their lives. It marked the moment when a part of their childhood and innocence was left behind. They remember it as the first time the outside world had encroached on their private lives, and the experience of growing up during wartime features significantly in their memories of childhood. For the next four years children like Beatrice Curtis Brown and A.L. Rowse were members of a society at war. They were not shielded from its dramas, exempt from its hardships or immune to its tragedies. Children in Britain experienced the First World War alongside Britain's adults. They participated in wartime society in a myriad of ways: as active volunteers, as students of a wartime education, and as children at play who found a place for the war in their books, toys and games. Perhaps most significantly, they participated in it as the children of families separated by war. An analysis of the experience of children, therefore, provides a fresh perspective for the study of British society at war.

When Britain declared war on Germany in August 1914 it had a standing army of just 244,260 men. By the time the war ended in November 1918, 5,215,162 men had served in the British Army.[3] During over four years of war the families of these men faced significant social and economic dislocation, often enduring long periods of separation as men volunteered or were conscripted to fight. Despite this, support for the war remained strong and civilians were involved in all aspects of the home front war effort. The demands of war required the vast mobilisation of men as both soldiers and workers, while their wives, girlfriends, sisters and mothers worked in industry, on land, in hospitals and civil associations. As their parents were drawn into working for the war, so too were children, some serving as messengers or guards in public buildings and strategic locations, many, many more saving for war bonds and collecting vital materials for the war effort. But mobilisation for war was not just about physical mobilisation, and the 'war effort' was not just a physical effort; it required enormous mental participation as well. For the population of Britain to continue to support the war for over four years, there had to be imaginative engagement and organisational participation in the collective experience of being at war. It is this all-encompassing mobilisation that has been the focus of recent historians' attempts to understand the experience of 'total war' in 1914–1918, and it is through an understanding of the ways in which children experienced this mobilisation that this book hopes to contribute towards the debate.

The theory that a 'war culture' existed in all the warring nations of Europe was developed by Stéphane Audoin-Rouzeau and Annette Becker, who have described it as

> a collection of representations of the conflict which crystallised into a system of thought which gave the war its deep significance.[4]

Through the convergence of religious and secular ideologies, a 'war culture' developed in the combatant nations which permeated every aspect of daily life and sustained the military and civilian commitment to war. The acceptance of military engagement and social mobilisation was made possible in the belligerent nations because it seemed to most that it was not just the nation that was at stake but human civilisation itself.[5] The Great War was imagined by each side as a struggle between civilisation and barbarity, confirmed, it seemed, by the sheer number of atrocity stories on each side, some real, many more invented.[6] The populations engaged in the struggle believed that they were defending not only their family and community but also the values and beliefs at the heart of their nation. It was believed that it was only war itself that could rid the world of future war at the hands of the opposing aggressor.[7]

In the development of this theory, Audoin-Rouzeau and Becker reject the emphasis placed in the past on seeing the soldiers and civilians of the First World War as victims. They believe that this emphasis has obscured the essential question of 'why and how millions of Europeans and Westerners acquiesced in the war of 1914–18'.[8] Instead, Becker points to the widespread belief by all parties that God was on their side, and describes a process whereby even nonbelievers came to see the war as a crusade for civilisation.[9] Wartime spirituality, including traditional Christian practice and the revival of ancient superstitions and the belief in the supernatural, helped ordinary people face the agony of both temporary and permanent separation.[10]

Audoin-Rouzeau and Becker have also been amongst a group of historians demonstrating how the study of childhood in the belligerent countries provides a way of analysing a nation's war culture. They suggest that the representations of war offered by adults to children, through books, periodicals, toys and images used at home, at school and in church, allow us to understand what society wanted to communicate to its children about the war. They argue that these representations, whether suggested or imposed, are like the 'inner core' of a nation's war culture.[11] They identify the study of children's experience of war as an opportunity for understanding the national response to war, saying:

> The behaviour of children in the belligerent societies is a reliable yardstick of the extent of the spontaneously mobilised support of the war and the extreme, largely self-imposed tension that prevailed during the four-year conflict. The children's involvement is the symptom of the ways in which the Great War was a crusade.[12]

Audoin-Rouzeau and Becker's research on France suggests that, on the whole, it was felt that no aspect of the war should be concealed from children. In fact, the very opposite should be encouraged. The reasoning, they explain, was that, while war itself was evil, this war was a war from which good would emerge. This war would, in fact, be good for children, not only now but in the future, by educating future adults 'rid forever of the obligation to wage war'.[13]

French schools used the war to impose responsibility on children. The soldier's duty in warfare was held up as an example to inspire duty to work in the classroom. As in Britain, as we shall see, lessons in all subjects were linked to the war. However, its saturation of the curriculum meant that the war became an everyday matter and the propaganda aimed at children failed to maintain the initial tension over the four and a half years of war.[14] Similarly, the wartime disruption to school and family life meant that the discipline needed to achieve the total mobilisation of children was missing. The school system, Audoin-Rouzeau believes, was trying to mobilise childhood intellectually and morally, just as children were becoming harder to reach.[15]

More work has been done on children's lives and schooling in Italy, where Andrea Fava has looked at the involvement of Italian teachers and unions in the pro-war education of children both inside and outside the official classroom. Fava has shown how Italian children became the 'active witnesses and symbolic bearers of the idea of nationalism'.[16] Through dissemination of propagandist material and the involvement of schools in organising children's presence at wartime ceremonies, both schools and children's charitable institutions reassured the public that Italy's children were a 'precious "well" of new, strong patriotism'.[17] The existence of, and strength of support for, these children's charitable institutions, Fava believes, illustrate a broader phenomenon in the history of children's wartime significance. In Italy, supporting children through charitable organisations became an act of solicitude towards the soldiers themselves and acted as a 'symbol of the nation's gratitude towards their brothers at war'.[18]

War culture has been analysed in Canada by Susan R. Fisher in her study of children's literature on the First World War, both contemporary and modern. Fisher adopts Audoin-Rouzeau and Becker's analysis to claim that the facts and interpretations Canadians wanted to transmit to their children about the war are evident in Canadian wartime children's literature. She believes that the themes of children's literature suggest that adults hoped that the terrible costs of war could be offset by the values war had taught children. It was believed that, if Canadian children could learn, from the example of the soldiers and from their own involvement in war work, the true meaning of service and sacrifice – 'those two great watchwords invariably invoked in discussions of children and the war' – the struggle would not have been in vain.[19]

Fisher also builds on George Mosse's theory of the brutalising effects of the trivialisation of war in the combatant nations. Mosse has argued that the mobilisation of children for war antedated 1914 and that the popularity of tin soldiers and war games in Germany and of boys' adventure fiction in England points to an identification with the concept of warfare amongst children in pre-war Europe.[20] Mosse believes that the existence and popularity of children's toys, games and ephemera during the war itself helped to trivialise the war in people's minds, but that this trivialisation 'helped people to confront war, just as its glorification did'.[21] For Fisher, the narrative patterns employed in children's reading about the war were similarly trivialising; 'they subsumed the unspeakable horrors of mass death within familiar plot structures that guaranteed a happy or at least reassuring ending'.[22]

For George Mosse, this process of trivialisation, rendering the war commonplace and ordinary, began a process in the minds of the warring populations which led to what he terms the 'domestication' of modern war, to the acceptance of war as a natural part of political and social life.[23] Thus 'brutalised', the combatant populations emerged from the First World War dulled in their response to the importance of individual human life, making them more accepting of the possibility of future war.[24] Pierre Purseigle believes that, when Mosse's theory of brutalisation and Audoin-Rouzeau and Becker's concept of a 'war culture' are combined, the First World War takes on a new significance, and sees it as

the harbinger of the industrialized massacres of the Second World War, and as the midwife of the barbaric 'short twentieth century'.[25]

*   *   *

While war undoubtedly destroys human life, it can, and did in the case of Britain during the First World War, provide some unforeseen health benefits. Jay Winter has shown how, in fact, some of the worst features of urban poverty which lay behind the high death rates of late Victorian and Edwardian Britain were eliminated as a result of the war. Winter has shown that one of the most important demographic effects of the First World War was the compression of the class structure, so that the gap in survival chances between different classes and between different sections within classes was reduced.[26] It was the very young, particularly,

who were to benefit from the consequences of wartime interest in the
health of the civilian population. Britain saw a massive expansion in its
infant welfare work during the war. In 1914 local authorities employed
just 600 health visitors, but by 1918 that figure had more than quadru-
pled to 2,577.[27] Local authority spending on child welfare clinics also
rose from £96,000 to £279,000 between 1916 and 1918. This growth
in interest and spending on infant and child health has led Deborah
Dwork to conclude that

> the public and professional protective reaction towards the youngest
> members of society when putting at risk the lives of those on the
> verge of realising their potential and reaching productivity meant, in
> short, that war was good for babies.[28]

But this interest in infant and child health was not entirely brought on
by war, or, at least, not by the First World War. The declining birth rate
and fears over national efficiency in the years immediately preceding
the war had provoked research and legislation designed to promote the
health and welfare of Britain's future imperial leaders and workers. It was
Britain's poor performance in the South African War (1899–1902) that
prompted the 1904 Report of the Physical Deterioration Committee. The
report was significant, as it rejected the then popular eugenicists' view,
which argued that degenerative stock was responsible for the perceived
physical deterioration of the race. Instead, it put forward a more opti-
mistic neo-hygienist view, which stressed that improvements could be
made to the health of the population if attention was paid to the diet,
health and hygiene of young people.[29]

The welfare legislation of the Liberal government after its 1906 elec-
tion victory was in part a recognition of this view. The 1906 Education
(Provision of School Meals) Act and the 1907 Education (Administra-
tive Provisions) Act provided for the feeding and medical inspection of
school children, making the state partially responsible for the health
and welfare of the nation's children.

At the same time a new and exciting conception of the child was
developing in Britain. Eighteenth-century Rousseauian ideas about the
'naturalness' of childhood and the innocence of children were being
complemented by a growing understanding on the part of psychologists, psychoanalysts and the medical profession of children's particular
physical and mental development.[30] Under the influence of educational
psychology, schools began to develop more child-centred teaching
methods. Old methods of instruction were abandoned in favour of new

techniques based on the work of Friedrich Froebel, Johann Heinrich Pestalozzi and others, which encouraged children to discover learning for themselves rather than having it imposed on them by adults.

So, then, when war broke out in 1914, state and professional interest in children in Britain had never been higher. Children were seen as both the problem and the solution for the strength and security of the British Empire. The war reinforced this vision, but with an added urgency that placed children at the heart of a national desire to both physically and psychologically repair the damage of war. It was hoped to replace the 'lost generation' with a happier, healthier, better-educated new generation, ready and willing to rebuild a stronger Britain.

For children themselves, the war meant something different. It was at times the cause of both great grief and great excitement. It could mean the separation for years at a time from dearly loved fathers and brothers, or the opportunity to play an active role in helping the war effort through work as a Boy Scout or Girl Guide. It meant changes to life at home and at school, some welcomed and others much resented. It provided new inspiration for everything from schoolwork to private fantasy. Some children followed the events of war closely; most had some personal connection in the form of a friend or relative caught up in the fighting.

The experience of children and the ways in which they responded to their mobilisation for war is, therefore, a major focus in this book. Their experience is reconstructed as far as possible through personal testimony. Using their own words, both those written at the time in letters sent to friends and relatives and those set down later in autobiography, we can attempt to understand how children made sense of the war around them. Their contemporary writing tells us that children accepted the war into their own lives through their relationships with men fighting abroad. Confronted with the separation from fathers and brothers, children had no choice but to engage with the events and circumstances of war if they were to find any common ground on which to build a relationship with their absent relatives. For most this posed few problems, as fathers tried hard to make their war accessible to their children, who in turn were also becoming familiar with it through lessons at school and in the books they read and games they played.

Using autobiography, this book also explores wartime memories mediated by time and life experience, in which the author attempts to recall their childhood but is forced to see it through adult eyes. This allows us to glimpse the children's war, what excited and frightened them, what upset them and what they did not understand while suggesting ways in which those experiences shaped the individual telling the story.

*   *   *

Arthur Marwick, in the second edition of his influential *The Deluge* (1965/1991), a study of British society during the First World War, speculated on what aspects of the First World War researchers of the future might choose to investigate. He considers children, and writes:

> There is, I flatter myself, some logic in the notions of working-class, or female participation in war, but what about children? Can one talk of children's 'participation' in the war effort? – most children, some children? What exactly does happen to them? What, with respect to children, would constitute 'gains'?[31]

In *The Deluge* Marwick is concerned with the civilian population's participation in the war and the way in which he believes that participation led to the various economic and political gains that sections of British society, notably women and the working classes, experienced. This book does not attempt to apply Marwick's reasoning to the situation of children during the war, but his questions are still relevant. I *will* be talking of children's participation in the war, both through their active participation (cultivating allotments, sounding air-raids, saving war bonds and joining the Guides and Scouts, for instance) and also through their participation as consumers of the media and as students of a wartime education. However, it is not so much any 'gains' that children made, but, rather, the way in which their participation was achieved and what it came to mean to the children themselves, that is of interest here.

The large-scale participation of children in the home front war effort required both their physical and mental mobilisation. This was achieved deliberately, and via adult mediation, through their involvement with war work organised through schools and youth groups and through their education, both formally delivered through the curriculum and also absorbed through the books they read and the manufactured toys they played with. But children also mobilised themselves. Invented games and imaginative connections were made by children, alone and with each other, which contributed towards their understanding of the war and defined their relationship to it. It is this space between adult efforts at mobilisation and children's own interpretation of it that I am particularly interested in. How adults wanted to communicate with children about the war shows us their fears for the nations, their desires in terms of reconstruction and their preoccupations with regard to the state and nature of their children. How children responded to their parents, teachers, youth group leaders, authors and anyone else attempting to mediate the war to them shows us the extent to which adults achieved their goals, but also where they failed. The failure to deliver a specific message, or having that message understood in a different way, can show us where children's understanding differed from that of adults; what *their* preoccupations, fears and anxieties were. Thus, in terms of understanding how 'total war' affected the psyche of a nation, the exploration of children's mobilisation provides evidence on two fronts.

But who are these children, and how do we attempt to identify and understand them? Childhood, according to Anna Davin, is a social construction, varying from place to place and over time, and is defined in relation to adulthood. Children are subordinate to and dependent upon adults, and adults expect obedience and determine how children spend their time.[32] This book is interested in the way in which adults, both those whom children met in public, like teachers and youth leaders, and those who cared for them in their domestic life, wanted children to spend their time. This is important not only in considering how the war influenced children's daily experiences, but also in looking at how adults during 1914–1918 were preparing children to live in the post-war era of reconstruction. What did these adults, who controlled children's activities and directed what they read and learnt, want children to understand about the war and Britain's part in it? How did they want children to feel about Britain's allies and enemies, and, ultimately, how did these adults want young people to feel about their own position in society and the world at large?

Rather than defining childhood by age range, say between 5 and 16 or 18, I came to realise, as Davin suggests, that it is experience rather than age that identifies someone more strongly with childhood. A young person of 14 might still be at school, treated as a child by both their parents and teachers, or could be out at work full-time, no longer a dependent but a major contributor to the household economy. Because one of my main areas of interest is the ways in which adults directed children's attention to the war, I have chosen to concentrate only on children who are still treated as children by the adults around them. I therefore do not include children in full-time paid work or those who lied about their age to enlist in the army. I do, however, include children up to the age of 18 while they are in full-time education. In the context of the chapter on uniformed youth groups, this definition becomes more complicated.

Many of the members of such youth groups were in fact young people in full-time paid work, but in this context they have been included. I realise that this is an artificial definition and that young people at work or in the army deserve as much attention as those children who were not, but for the purposes of this book I am choosing to concentrate on those considered to be, and treated as, children.[33]

Discussing the idea of childhood in history, Carolyn Steedman has reflected on both real children and, often, literary depictions of children. She has explored social responses to questions concerning children as well as cultural understandings of what childhood represents for adults trying to recapture their own pasts. Describing the search for the past, both the public historical past and the individual's personal past, Steedman has focused on autobiography. Autobiography is one medium for the individual's narrative of growth and development, and these often begin with descriptions of childhood. The remembered childhood in autobiography, Steedman explains, has become the dominant way of telling the story of how one came to be the way one is, and she compares this narrative of self-discovery with the narrative of 'history':

> In the practices of history and modern autobiographical narration, there is the assumption that *nothing goes away*; that the past has deposited all of its traces, somewhere, somehow (though they may be, in particular cases, difficult to retrieve).[34]

Despite this similarity between the idea of history and the idea of childhood, Steedman also believes that there is a contradiction inherent in the search for each. Steedman argues that the study of history offers the fantasy that what is being searched for may be found, that, by reconstructing all the evidence left behind, the past may reappear. The search for childhood, on the other hand, Steedman believes, is hopeless. For Steedman, the very idea of childhood symbolises something that is gone and that

> the very search for the past in each of us changes the past as we go along, so that the lost thing is not the same now, as it was before.[35]

Much of the way we understand the modern self to be is as a product of our childhood, with our child self always within us. For Steedman, this means that the search for childhood, or the idea of childhood, becomes in some ways our search for ourselves. Between 1900 and 1920 Freudian psychoanalysis developed many nineteenth-century debates about the idea that at the core of an individual's psychic identity was her or his own lost past, or childhood. It was through this theorising of childhood that the idea of the 'unconscious' was born, and by the 1920s had been quite widely disseminated.[36]

The children in this study were growing up as Sigmund Freud's ideas about childhood and the unconscious were becoming influential. This was a time, then, when new ideas about the importance of childhood were being recognised, not only in terms of securing the future of the race through raising healthy children, but also as new psychodynamic theories of human nature were placing childhood at the centre of meaning. In considering the mobilisation of children, therefore, it is important to note that an understanding of the importance of childhood experiences in shaping the adult self (the adults of the future) was beginning to be recognised by psychoanalysts, psychologists, doctors and teachers all working with children at this time.

So how were these adults of the future shaped by their childhood experiences? By considering the autobiographies of those who lived through the First World War as children and then recalled their childhood as adults, we can come closest to trying to understand the influence of the war on their lives. But there are problems inherent in the use of such memories. Graham Dawson believes that, while the remembering adult is, in a way, putting her or himself back inside her or his childhood self, this discrepancy between past investment and the current social context renders the memory open to fresh examination and interpretation. This creates a 'double consciousness, both "inside" and "outside" childhood', where the memory of how one felt as a child is questioned and evaluated within the context of the adult present.[37]

This point is interesting when you consider the number of autobiographers who recorded their childhood memories of the First World War on the eve of, and during, the Second World War. The earlier war looms large in their minds because they feel they are almost living through it all again. Indeed, even for those who wrote after the Second World War, it is possible that their earlier memories were altered by the experience. The particularly vivid memories of air-raids recalled by many may owe much to the far more widespread threat from the air that those who lived through the Second World War experienced.

In his book *Soldier Heroes – British Adventure, Empire and the Imagining of Masculinities* (1994), Graham Dawson has looked at the image of the soldier hero as an idealised form of masculinity within Western culture. For Dawson, although masculinities are lived out in the flesh, they are created in the imagination. Military virtues such as strength, aggression, courage and endurance are often seen as the natural characteristics of manhood, and the ultimate display of these qualities is only possible through battle. Through his depiction as an adventure hero in literature and on screen, the soldier has become the 'quintessential figure of masculinity'.[38] The sources I have used confirm Dawson's argument that it is through childhood exposure to the soldier hero that young boys learn some of the characteristics that typify the male persona. During the First World War, children, and particularly boys, were surrounded by militaristic images and messages. Chapter 3, 'War Imagined', looks specifically at children's fiction, toys and leisure pursuits, many of which concerned the re-creation of the war itself. Battles and military leaders were fictionalised in literature, miniature copies of military uniforms were available in the shops, and, as described by some of the autobiographers, children's imaginative play also echoed the war going on in the adult world.

In the final section of his book Dawson traces the part played by these images of the soldier hero in his own developing masculinity. To do this, Dawson re-examines his childhood and discusses both the way in which memory helps in shaping the individual, and also the way in which memory itself is shaped by social context. In remembering his own childhood, Dawson produced detailed descriptions of past events, kinds of play, and the forms of toys and games, and of the imaginative investments he once made in them. These investments from the past, however, reappear in a quite different context in the present, and Dawson's thoughts about the remembered past are in some ways close to Steedman's:

> Memory is never simply a 'record' of the past made 'at the time', but is a constant process of reworking, driven by the needs of the present. Any account of our own childhood experience based on memory is necessarily an adult evaluation of that experience and a reflection on our own cultural formation.[39]

If what we want is a 'record' of the past 'made at the time', despite its strengths, autobiography clearly has some limitations. Letters, on the other hand, offer us the chance to consider the contemporary writing of wartime families. Although they have sometimes been dismissed by historians of the war because it was believed wartime censorship prevented men from communicating truthfully with their families,[40] recent work by historians including Martha Hanna, Christa Hämmerle and Michael Roper has shown how important letters were in maintaining and strengthening the bonds with home.[41] The wartime letters of children and their fathers, brothers, uncles and others offer us a glimpse into the daily lives of families at war and allow us a chance to understand how they continued to function as a unit of support for each other despite the distance in both location and experience.

Martha Hanna has used French wartime correspondence to argue that military and civilian France were 'not isolated, mutually indifferent communities', but, instead, continued to be intimately connected to each other via the mail they sent and received, keeping 'the horrors of combat vividly present to mind and the refuge of home never entirely remote'.[42] But she also argues that the study of wartime letters can do more than just reveal insights into how men retained their civilian identity and how women continued to provide loving support for their husbands. The study of family correspondence allows us to engage with 'the history of affect and emotion as fundamental components of war'.[43] While it is accepted that the almost universal experience of loss during the First World War produced a post-war Europe burdened down with grief, Hanna argues that historians have not understood the journey towards that grief. Survivors mourning those they had loved had forged, strengthened and maintained that love in their letters. Hanna believes that letters, which are neither exclusively masculine nor wholly introspective but are 'simultaneously dialogical and intimate', allow us to understand how men and women shared in the experience of war and supported each other through it. But to truly understand why letters were treasured by each side we must look beyond their testimonial content and 'analyse their affective and emotional functions and implications'.[44]

Michael Roper has also used letters to try to understand emotional survival in wartime. His study of the wartime letters of soldiers and their mothers has led him to conclude that historians must try to do more than just consider letters as cultural forms. In looking for evidence of the horrors of trench life, Roper believes, historians have been too concerned with the semantics of language. They have not understood the 'emotions carried through words', meaning that the experience of trench warfare has been viewed at one remove.[45] Roper believes historians need to do more than just consider the collective memories of war, the changes and continuities in the representations of war, and the social expectations surrounding death and mourning. If the emotional history of the war is to be about more than cultural conventions, Roper believes that, when reading personal accounts of the horrors of war, historians must take seriously the sensation of 'nameless dread' so that they are 'not locking away the pain of the past, but trying to digest and contain it'.[46]

The extent and content of children's wartime correspondence suggests that letters provided an essential medium through which children came to understand the war. At school they were taught letter writing and were encouraged to correspond with soldiers they did not know as a lesson in citizenship. This correspondence sometimes produced fledgling friendships which sustained men, some of whom, in the case of Australian soldiers serving far from home, may have had little other local contact, throughout the years of war. For other children, it was letters that allowed them to remain emotionally close to their absent fathers and brothers. From family correspondence it is clear that British soldiers remained connected to the domestic world of their children, and that children were often invited to leave the imaginative confines of home to join their fathers in the trenches.

*   *   *

In 1914 one young officer, Julian Grenfell, who was later to die of wounds in France, wrote to his mother during the First Battle of Ypres:

> I adore war. It is like a big picnic without the objectlessness of a picnic. I've never been so happy or so well.[47]

Grenfell, like so many other young officers, was the product of a public school education in which the traditions of loyalty to House and School, the glorification of games and the classical education received meant that, almost universally, public school boys flocked to the recruiting stations throughout the war. The public schools expounded the importance of service to empire and the superiority of the British gentleman, while the influence of a Victorian revival of medieval chivalry and late nineteenth-century romanticism created a cult of youth and death whereby young men dedicated to duty and self-sacrifice were desperate to prove themselves on the battlefields.[48]

Outside the public schools, children's books, and particularly boys' adventure fiction, continued the traditions of 'muscular Christianity' made popular by Thomas Hughes' hugely influential *Tom Brown's Schooldays* (1857). Such fiction passed on the image of the robust and healthy English public schoolboy, as one who loved danger and always played fair. But boys educated within the public school system were not the only recipients of this message; its ideas and values were disseminated more widely through comics and magazines, led by the *Boys' Own Paper*.

Boys' adventure stories, in which the heroes displayed the very best of British character, began to take on an overtly imperialist tone by the end of the nineteenth century. James Walvin sees such children's fiction as being extremely influential, both commercially and in shaping the historical and social perceptions of a generation of schoolboys. He believes that, as the political and diplomatic conflicts of the Edwardian age were incorporated into children's fiction, a new generation of protagonists were emerging, eager to live out their fictional fantasies.[49] During the war itself, boys' adventure fiction continued to be popular and quickly responded to the new international conflict to provide tall tales of heroic acts in battle on the Western Front and elsewhere.

Sally Mitchell has argued that girls' fiction became more 'manly' in the years leading up to the First World War as authors capitalised on the opportunity to write for the 'new' girls of Edwardian Britain.[50] For Mitchell, the period between 1880 and 1915 represents a brief moment when both working-class and middle-class girls increasingly occupied a separate culture. She claims that the introduction of compulsory schooling, changes in child labour laws and changes to the employment patterns and opportunities open to girls of all classes meant that many more girls had some 'period of transition between "child at home" and the assumption of wholly adult responsibilities'.[51] The fiction aimed at these girls allowed them, at least mentally, to imagine life as a boy, and during the First World War there were many opportunities for more active roles for girls on paper. Heroines are given the opportunity to work on the land and in factories, and some even make it to France as military drivers. They work hard, catch spies and rescue men while at the same time retaining all of their 'womanly' dignity, earning them the admiration and occasional love of their male support cast.

Militarist and imperialist themes were not only to be found in children's fictional literature; in classrooms and textbooks across the country educationalists and teachers were using the school curriculum to inculcate young people with specific ideas and attitudes towards Britain's place in the world. As much history and geography teaching at this time focused on the examination of the works and achievements of great men, John MacKenzie feels it is significant that one of the dramatic shifts in emphasis was in the attitudes of school texts to specific historical figures. He notes that from the 1890s onwards, warlike figures were increasingly venerated, while those who did nothing to advance the empire were often condemned. Within the texts certain periods were glossed over – the Civil War, the slave trade and times of sexual licence – while patriotism, militarism, adulation of the monarchy and imperial expansion became the textbooks' major concerns.[52]

To impart the message of patriotism and national service, the lives of great soldiers and significant figures in the expansion of the British Empire were held up as examples to school children of the sort of qualities to be emulated. The ideal hero combined piety, adventure and military prowess in the best traditions of Christian militarism that developed in the 1860s and 1870s. With warfare seen in a positive light, war stories constituted a significant percentage of English and history 'readers' at the end of the nineteenth century. John MacKenzie points out that, in the 1899 Revised Code, 12 out of the 30 stories from 1688 to the present for Standard V were devoted to war and war heroes. By 1911, The Cambridge University Press readers contained 24 military figures out of 40 historical personalities selected for study.[53]

The significance of this emphasis in the school curriculum on warfare and military heroism cannot be underestimated when considering children's responses to the Great War. With war being taught at worst as a necessary evil, and at best as a chance for Britain to assert her physical and moral superiority over her enemies, it is unsurprising that children were often as enthusiastic about Britain's participation in the war as other sections of the population. Even if they did not possess the background knowledge to know why Britain had gone to war, they would have been well versed in the importance of upholding British honour and serving the flag, ensuring that military recruiters of the future would have a ready and willing supply of volunteers.

The Boy Scout movement, founded by the former soldier and war hero Robert Baden-Powell, also made a substantial contribution to the preparation of a generation of boys for military service. The war gave the Scout movement the opportunity to prove itself a dependable auxiliary service in a time of national emergency. In effect, this had been one of the aims behind the initial formation of the Scout movement; to be prepared to contribute towards the defence and maintenance of the British Empire.[54] As such, the Boy Scout organisation made a significant contribution to sustaining and building on the patriotic and militaristic training of young people in Britain that was begun in the classroom and carried on through fiction.

Research for Chapter 4, 'Children in Uniform', shows that children in youth groups were keen to undertake unpaid war work in their spare time and after school. Girls in female youth groups also relished the opportunity to serve the war effort as it gave them the chance to break away from the home-centred, domestic activities of the pre-war years and take on more public roles as everything from messengers in public buildings to working in hospitals. Sally Mitchell has even suggested that girls' hunger to wear uniform and join in boys' military games may have been a subliminal reaction to the then popular anti-suffrage contention that anyone who could not help to defend their country had no right to share in its decision making.[55]

Do all these children in uniform prove that Britain became militarised during the First World War? Not according to Gerard DeGroot, who defines militarism as 'the domination of government and society by military elites, a tendency to overvalue military power and the dissemination of military values into wider society'.[56] Neither the first nor the second definition can be said to apply to Britain, according to DeGroot, but military values did spread into wider society. However, the 'militarism' evidenced by uniformed youth groups, boys' adventure fiction and the ethos of the public schools was not designed to prepare Britain for war or to turn its schoolboys into soldiers. Instead, DeGroot believes that its primary aim was social control and the lure of youth away from the football grounds and street corners where they could descend into hooliganism.[57] Despite the fact that over 40 per cent of all male adolescents belonged to some form of youth organisation by 1914,[58] DeGroot believes we should not assume that any military intent was successfully passed on. He believes that boys probably listened to what they were interested in and ignored the rest. They joined youth groups and read novels because they were fun: 'A bit of Christian indoctrination and some innocent drill was probably a small price to pay for the opportunity to play a good game of football on a real pitch with a real ball or to read a cracking good story'.[59]

While that may be true in general terms when thinking about boys' motivation for joining youth groups, I will show that sometimes boys were so keen to use their military preparation that they actually went beyond what they were instructed and allowed to do. Evidence that children had their own attitudes to the war can be seen in the fact that they sometimes went against the instructions of their leaders, putting themselves in danger, because of the desire to 'help' the war effort. This suggests that children's mobilisation was thorough and did not just come from one source. Inspiration to become involved may have come from any number of places: fiction, school texts, news reports, toys, games and play; but also through the family connection, the desire to emulate the bravery of older brothers or fathers.

This book considers children's relationship to the First World War, how they experienced it, how they understood it and how they responded to it. It asks why and how children's minds and bodies were mobilised for war by adult society and considers the ways in which children mobilised themselves, physically, mentally and emotionally, and their motivation for doing so. The chapters 'Families at War' and 'War Imagined' look at how the war affected children at home, how it altered their family relationships, changed the food they could eat, the toys that they played with and books that they read. 'Families at War' uses autobiography and family correspondence to understand how and why children worked so hard to sustain relationships with men separated from them for so long. It addresses how parents and children managed to continue to operate as family units despite the years of separation, and asks how both came to interpret and accept the war as an integral part of their relationship with each other. It also explores the process of loss and grief for families, and children in particular. Over 350,000 children lost their fathers during the First World War, and, with a total of 722,785 British servicemen who died, many thousands more would have lost brothers, cousins, uncles, friends and neighbours.[60]

'War Imagined' uses commercially produced children's toys, games and books to consider how all-pervading war culture was in children's lives. Its use as inspiration for stories, board games, card games, model figures and props for imaginative play shows how keen adults were to share the themes of war with their children. But the commercial success of the more cheaply produced toys and magazines, afforded by children themselves from modest pocket money, is evidence of the children's own desire for such objects. And when children invented games which required no manufactured elements we begin to understand how they interpreted and adapted that war culture for use in their own private fantasy.

In 'Children in Uniform' and 'War in the Classroom' we consider how teachers and youth group leaders harnessed children's genuine interest in the war to encourage learning and help with motivation. These chapters also look at how children's energies were channelled into working for the war effort, how they became involved in everything from knitting clothes, collecting money, making bandages and splints to working in government departments and guarding bridges and reservoirs. These chapters focus on the way adults wanted children to interpret the lessons of the war, how they wanted children to understand the sacrifices that had been made for them and the importance of accepting their role as responsible citizens of the future. But evidence for these chapters show that in schools and youth groups children were not simply the passive receptors of adult indoctrination. Children brought their own interpretation of the war with them to school and acted on their own determination when serving as Scouts and Guides. What we can consider in these chapters is how and where adults and children were in agreement over the war and where their understandings differed. By considering children in these settings we can explore how their mobilisation was achieved through institutions, sometimes under the direction of government and other times through the organising efforts of social reformers. Here we see direct interaction between the state and the nation's children and can consider the extent and ways in which children's mobilisation was achieved.

By using a combination of official documents, school texts, youth group material, literature and children's ephemera, these adult constructions of the war, produced for children, will be explored to identify ideas about the child in Edwardian society. By considering how adults tackled the subject of the war, we can begin to grasp how they wanted the future generation to understand the adult world. Through their depiction of the conflict and the way they interpreted Britain's role in it, we can reflect on how adult society understood itself and hoped to be understood by the coming generation. In contrast to this, by looking at autobiography and children's letters we can attempt to understand how this war became a part of individuals' lives. We can consider how children felt about events over which they had no control, but which changed their lives completely. These sources allow us to try to discover how young people reconstructed the messages they received from adults to develop their own understanding of the war.

What all of these sources show is that the war entered every aspect of children's lives. It dominated much of their teaching and school experience, it was the focus of their extra-curricular activities and they enjoyed it as a source of entertainment in literature and play. Perhaps even more significantly, it dominated their life at home through the absence, both temporary and permanent, of fathers and brothers and through the way in which it preoccupied those adults left behind. I believe the study of children's lives provides a unique perspective on British society during the First World War. It lets us get to the very essence of how Britain's adults perceived the war and allows us to explore the methods society used to communicate with itself. Because children had no official voice through which to respond to the message of adults, as opposed to the way in which difference of opinion between adults could play out in parliament, in the press or in the street, that communication at first appears one-sided. We are able to build up quite a broad picture of the ways in which adults filtered the war for children, unchallenged in the public sphere by the children themselves. This demonstrates how the war culture began and the ways in which it developed as the war went on.

But we can also, through the study of children's writing and through their personal memories, begin to understand how that war culture touched individuals. Children absorbed the messages delivered by adults, but also contributed to that war culture by responding in ways unimagined by their parents and teachers. Playing imaginary war games or remembering a favourite childhood book is evidence of the way in which war entered the popular imagination. For children it may not have been about the creation of an understanding of war based around the notion of crusade, but it was one based on the idea of defensive love.[61] Children imagined what their fathers and brothers were experiencing and acted it out for themselves or loved books which described it. They took the opportunity to contribute in the only ways they could. At school and in their youth groups they worked harder, took on more responsibility and shared in the preoccupations of the adults around them. They built strategies for coping with the war and ways of maintaining their relationships which sustained them through wartime but also acted to give the war a central position in their memories of childhood.

2
Families at War

Molly Keen's elder brothers, Jack and Percy, both enlisted in the army as soon as they were old enough to. Molly remembers her mixed emotions every time they returned home on leave:

> The joy and excitement when they arrived quite unexpectedly was overwhelming. Those seven days went oh so quickly, then came the dreaded time for departure... How we hated that awful moment for goodbye not knowing if we would see them again.[1]

The Keens were a close family, living in Hounslow on the outskirts of London, and this separation from her two beloved brothers brought joy and pain to Molly as they left and returned several times during the course of the war. The First World War required the vast deployment of troops, first through voluntary enlistment and then, after 1916, through conscription. After that any man between the ages of 18 and 41, considered to be medically fit and not exempt on occupational grounds, was deemed to have enlisted. This meant that huge numbers of children were separated from their fathers and sometimes their brothers for several years during the war.

Having a father involved in the war effort was a cause of great pleasure and pride for some children. Edith Hall's father was in the Royal Army Medical Corps during the war, and while he was away her mother lodged girls from the nearby munitions factories (canary girls). Hall remembers the impact these girls had on her childhood and how she associated her father with the young men they were seeing away at the Front:

> The Canaries must have been with us for about three or four years and were no doubt a great influence on my formative years and it

pleased me that I received pretty French postcards from my Daddy as they also did from their soldier boys.[2]

For Hall, having a father involved with the war held a certain sense of relief and allowed her to identify with the older girls she so admired who were living with the family at the time. Hall's father was captured during the war and spent some years in a prisoner of war camp, but, rather than being upset by this, she remembers that:

> I was secretly glad that he had been taken prisoner because my friend had been told by her father that RAMC men weren't really in the war and didn't face the dangers of the fighting men.[3]

It was important for Hall that her father faced danger like the fathers of her friends and like the boyfriends of the munitions workers who lodged with them. But for other children there could be nothing worse than being parted from a father. Arthur Jacobs was deeply affected every time his father, a Post Office worker, had to return to the army after a period of leave:

> It was hard to tell which of us was the more wretchedly unhappy – mother or me. In a way it was a relief when he was out of reach, because some of those Sunday evenings when the three of us walked through the mocking sunshine down through Frognal to Fortune Green, where he would catch a bus for Woolwich, were the unhappiest I have ever known. We were all brightly cheerful, of course, and probably no outsider could have sensed the underlying misery; for father rarely showed signs of any kind of emotion and insisted that mother and I followed suit.[4]

An only child, and only seven years old when war broke out, Jacobs was obviously deeply affected by the separation from his father and remembers that:

> The worst part of all was walking back up from Frognal with mother – springtime and the Hampstead we both had known for all our lives, and shared, of course, with father. Walking back with lagging footsteps, I making useless, inane remarks in an effort to be funny, and trying desperately hard not to think about the put-off homework awaiting me back in that strangely empty flat, with father's books and pipes and other personal belongings still around the place to rub their own peculiar salt into fresh wounds.[5]

For many children the war meant a permanent separation from family members. Joseph Armitage's brother had joined the Army in January 1915, and in the June of that year his family received notification that he was one of the 230,000 Allied troops killed at Gallipoli.[6]

> I shall always remember the morning that the long buff coloured envelope came by the early post. Mother sat down and opened it then her face seemed to freeze like a mask. I remember asking her what the letter was about, after a while she said in a strange quiet voice – 'George is dead, he's been killed'.
>
> She said nothing else for what seemed like hours, she just sat there at the end of the long white deal table staring straight in front of her.[7]

The death of George meant that for some time, until his war pension came through, the family was in financial difficulties. Armitage remembers how his mother had to go to one after another of her relatives to borrow money and believes that that experience, coupled with the loss of her son, changed his mother completely. He felt that she seemed to hold a grudge and began to treat everyone with suspicion and distrust, shunning her neighbours and almost all her relatives.

The presence of so many war widows and orphans in British society during and after the First World War became one of the most symbolic legacies of the war. Their sacrifice was much vaunted by recruiters, politicians and the press in attempts to shame other men into enlistment and keep the threat of defeat in the public mind. Erika Kuhlman argues that war widows (and by extension orphans) performed honoured roles as living, patriotic symbols of self-sacrifice to the nation.[8] But they also represented a danger to morale if their individual and collective mourning was not channelled towards national pride.

For Armitage's mother, the loss of her elder son had a profound impact on her relationship with her younger son. He explains:

> I was not allowed out of her sight, for the next two years I was almost a prisoner at home, it was a relief to go to school and mix with other boys.[9]

Armitage remembers hearing other people tell his mother that, as he was young (in fact only seven years old when his brother was killed), he would soon get over the death, but he felt that it was not that easy.

> More especially was this so because mother had developed a habit of talking to herself when she was alone and I was (or she thought that

I was asleep) or otherwise out of earshot. If there had been another child, or someone else that I could have talked to, it would have been a great comfort to me, but all that I could do was listen and say nothing.[10]

C.H. Rolph, the son of a police sergeant, was 13 when war broke out and remembers feeling deeply troubled when his older brother attested under the Derby Scheme, a voluntary registration system designed to prove the need for conscriptions.[11] His brother became a member of the Honourable Artillery Company:

By September 1917 he was in France, and my heart and my alter ego went with him. The occasion of his departure to France remains in my memory indelibly, distressing me to this day.[12]

Rolph was close to his elder brother, making his identification with him all the more powerful. He felt that he too should be in France, sharing the experiences and fate of his sibling. In a close family, where what happens to one has a profound effect on all, this separation must have been particularly traumatic. At this time in the war the British were heavily involved in the third battle of Ypres – Passchendaele, which killed 268,000 British troops.[13] The casualty figures reported in the press were appalling and those back in England were beginning to realise the full horror of the battle. When the time came for his brother to leave, Rolph remembers that the reaction of his father greatly surprised him at the time:

My father knew only too well that anyone 'going up the line' at that time stood a poor chance of surviving, and when Harold said goodbye I was severely shaken to see my father embrace him in tears. Just as though they were both foreigners.[14]

Arthur Jacobs has described how some of the teachers at his junior school in London dealt with children who were going through some extremely difficult times:

Children in Mr Hill's class (to which I was soon promoted en route for the scholarship class) brought their domestic burdens to school to be shared. Fathers and brothers were 'missing' – fathers and brothers were dead. Some of the children seemed stunned and uncomprehending; others – sensitive and afraid – were told to put their heads on their arms and 'rest'. Sometimes their sobbings became unbearable and a prelude to the despairing youngsters being sent home – to what additional misery?[15]

So how did these families, separated for so long and under such stressful and dangerous circumstances, maintain their bonds? How did children and their fathers compensate for their separation and sustain each other throughout the long years of war? With the exception of periods of leave, the only form of communication open to families was the letter, and throughout the war this is how the millions of children in Britain with a father serving in the army continued their family life.

By 1917 the Army on the Western Front alone was sending home 8,150,000 letters a week, and over the course of the war it has been estimated that the British Army's main postal depot in Britain handled 2,000 million letters and papers as well as 114 million parcels.[16] Within that vast volume of mail are the letters of children to their fathers and those their fathers sent in return. The ordinary men who made up the majority of British troops during the First World War had no previous experience of fighting or army life. They left behind children with no benchmark against which to measure their feelings and anxieties about being separated from their fathers for so long.

During the war the bonds of men and their children were maintained through letters as each side attempted to keep the other involved in their lives despite the separation in both distance and experience. Children did this by reminding their fathers of the world they had left behind. They told them tales of home and school, of friends and family, attempting to situate their fathers back into the centre of their own domestic landscape. Fathers, on the other hand, used both domestic imagery and fantasy to create a new reality for themselves on paper that could be both exciting and safe for their children. They had to liken their surroundings to ones with which their children were familiar, but then they employed their imagination to create scenes in which their dual identity as both parent and soldier could coexist. They did this both for their children and for themselves as a way of reconciling their new reality with their old. As such, these letters provide a fascinating insight into the emotional history of soldiers at war.

The notion that soldiers were isolated from those at home through their experience serving in the trenches has been challenged in recent years by historians pointing to the continuities between civilian and military life and to the attempts made by soldiers to maintain links to family and community at home. It has been argued that, rather than hiding the realities of warfare from their families, men were often happy to talk in person or through their letters about their experiences in the fighting line.[17] Rather than feeling alienated from their families because those at home lacked any real understanding of what the war was really like, it seems that men were keen to share their experiences with their families and were able to overcome the British Army's censorship methods to do this.

Censorship of letters had been introduced at the outbreak of war, prohibiting men from discussing a range of subjects regarded as possibly useful to the enemy. These included comments on the effects of hostile fire, the physical and moral condition of the troops and details of defensive work.[18] Letters to family and friends from the non-commissioned had to be submitted to the scrutiny of their commanding officer. Officers, on the other hand, were expected to censor themselves, although their mail was still liable to be read by the regimental censor before being sent on to England. However, as Helen McCartney has pointed out, in reality the practice of censorship could vary greatly between battalions, and much depended on the attitude of the individual censor.[19] The vast bulk of correspondence meant that censorship was, at best, patchy.[20]

The effect of censorship on the content of letters sent home is difficult to tell. Would men, freed to write as they please, have told those at home more of the details of what they were experiencing? We cannot know, although one of the letters in this chapter does suggest that the knowledge that their mail was to be read by a third party did curb some men's enthusiasm for writing as well as the content of their message. However, men also recognised the impact of their news on those at home, and that may arguably have placed just as much of a constraint on them as did formal censorship.[21] Letters from England, on the other hand, were uncensored, and some men got around the rules by giving their mail to friends to post when home on leave. This also meant that letters sent to soldiers were uncensored, and in this way men learnt of the true extent of food shortages and bomb damage from their families at home.[22]

But the letters sent by soldiers and their families were about more than just keeping up with news, and the writing and receiving of a letter came to represent very different things depending on the circumstances. To the soldiers at the Front, the letters they received provided messages of love and support that were recognised by the army as being essential for morale. The letters they sent were the way in which men maintained their relationships with their wives, girlfriends, parents and children. They were the means by which the men could attempt to escape their surroundings and recover, albeit temporarily, their pre-war, independent selves.

For those at home, most often the wives, mothers and sisters of soldiers, the act of writing a letter was the way in which they showed their continuing devotion to their absent husbands, sons and brothers. Parcels of clothing and tobacco were also sent as the women attempted to continue their role of providing for the physical well being of their families. Early in the war, before food shortages had really begun to be felt in Britain, parcels of food were also regularly dispatched by families of all classes. Working-class wives and mothers baked cakes and pies with whatever spare food they could manage, while richer families could order luxury hampers from the major department stores to be sent straight out to their soldier's regiment.

Perhaps most importantly, receiving a letter from a soldier was, for those left at home, a continuing sign of life. With communication lines often disrupted and newspaper reports, particularly after major battles, unreliable, a letter proved to those at home that their soldier was still alive.

The absence of a letter, for both those at home and those at the Front, often caused alarm and confusion. Delays caused by troop movements or a disruption of the mail service could leave both parties fearful and confused. Those at home worried that their soldier had been injured or killed, while the soldiers themselves often worried that they were being forgotten by those they had left behind.[23]

The British High Command appreciated the role of mail in maintaining morale in wartime, and a regular mail service was maintained throughout the war. Behind the lines, men could take advantage of the recreation huts established by churches and groups like the Scouts and Guides, which always supplied free stationery as well as a comfortable place to compose or read a letter. Indeed, many of the letters included in this chapter are written on headed, YMCA or equivalent paper. Even without appropriate stationery men still found a way to write home. Other letters read for this chapter were written on scraps of paper, torn from notebooks and diaries, and penned in anything from crayon to fountain pen.

When men moved up the lines, the practicalities of writing home got harder. Not only were writing materials and a surface to write on harder to find, but what it was possible to say was limited as well. The army's answer to this second problem was the Field Service Postcard. The pre-printed card allowed men to communicate a limited amount of information to their families by choosing the option from a list of several that best described their circumstances. The remaining options could be deleted, but no additional message was allowed. Thus, men in front line trenches could let their families know whether or not they were well, and whether they had received any mail recently, but could give away nothing as to how they were feeling or what action they were taking part in.

These cards amused many at the time, and have become a much lampooned image of the war because of the way in which they allowed the sender no opportunity for individuality in their expression of anything from good to really dreadful news. Paul Fussell has described them as being the first widespread example of a 'form' – that type of document which 'uniquely characterises the modern world'.[24] Fussell also points out the implicit optimism in the postcards, saying:

> One paid for the convenience of using the postcard by adopting its cheerful view of things, by pretending to be in a world where belated mail and a rapidly healing wound are the worst that can happen, and where there is only one thinkable direction one can go – to the rear.[25]

But adopting a cheerful view of things was not something soldiers did only when using a Field Service Postcard. Understating the horrors they were witnessing and the risks they were taking was something many soldiers did in their letters, especially when writing to their children. This chapter will explore the ways in which men's style of writing reflected their own feelings towards participation in the war as well as their attitudes towards their children. These men were constructing their war experience on paper for their children, and we must try to understand the part this construction played in helping them reconcile their roles as both soldier and father.

The letters in this chapter are part of the Imperial War Museum's collection of documents that have been donated over the years since the war ended.[26] Sometimes these letters are part of a larger collection of one family's correspondence, often accompanied by detailed biographical information and other artefacts like medals and photographs. On other occasions the archive simply holds individual letters, with little or no accompanying biographical detail; where biographical information is available it has been included, but it is often incomplete or largely missing.

With all types of letter, I found far more letters sent by soldiers than letters sent to them. This is because the survival of letters sent to the Front was much more precarious than for those sent home. They may have been lost in the course of battle, or discarded by a soldier on the move. Letters sent to Britain, on the other hand, were usually treasured and saved, not only by family members but also, as we shall see in a later chapter, by individual children who valued their messages from 'their' soldier.

All of the letters in this chapter were exchanged by children and their fathers or other close male relatives. Many of the letters represent intimate portraits of family life and give valuable clues to Edwardian issues of parenting and the role of the father within the family. Many of the sets of correspondence do not begin until 1916 or 1917, suggesting that these family men did not volunteer to fight but were eventually conscripted into the army and forced to leave their families.

As family units were broken up by war, letters became the main channel through which communication between husbands and wives and fathers and children could be maintained. Some men, who had perhaps never written before, wrote regularly to their wives and children, attempting to be a partner and parent from abroad. Others were clearly unfamiliar with the practice or lacked the confidence to write lengthy regular letters. Without detailed knowledge of the educational background of these correspondents it is difficult to be certain whether reticence in writing was a result of lack of ability, or simply a lack of inclination on the writer's part. Working-class soldiers would have attended elementary school at least, but many perhaps had had little need or opportunity to compose letters, and were, therefore, hindered in their attempts to maintain contact with those at home. That is not to say, however, that all working-class fathers struggled to correspond with their children. On the contrary, most of the letters in this chapter are from men serving in other ranks, and it is often the letters from officers that are the most uncommunicative.

Because we have only a very small proportion of the millions of letters sent between fathers and their children, we cannot draw any general conclusions about the differences between working, middle or upper-class family relationships. It could be that working-class families, whose children lived at home and were schooled locally, were less used to being separated and therefore wrote more often. Or perhaps it was the case that officers were more conscious of their duty to keep up morale at home and so wrote only in general, positive terms to their children. What we do know is that these letters have survived the intervening years because they meant something to the people who received them. They were sent and kept by families that loved each other. They were treasured and eventually deposited in the national archive because those who kept or found them recognised their importance as testimony to how ordinary people responded to extraordinary conditions.

Children, particularly older children, often wrote weekly to their fathers, encouraged by mothers and teachers to keep their fathers up to date about their lives and to show their support for the war. Younger children were also included in the letter writing cycle, with fathers writing them separate letters intended to be read out to them by their mothers. In return mothers penned letters dictated by their children, or composed ones themselves for the very young. The arrival of a letter often became a family event, with everyone gathering together to hear the news, as men with little time to write asked children to share their letters with their siblings.

Some fathers wrote to their children individually and often, others hardly at all, preferring to send love to them as a line at the end of their letters to their wives. Some fathers spoke at length about the war and the conditions in which they were living, while others dwelt entirely on family matters, responding to the news from home. None of the letters I have read, written by fathers home to children, mention specific instances of violence or death, although some do mention guns and shells. There are far fewer surviving letters sent by children to their fathers, but from the replies sent back to England it is sometimes possible to gauge the tone and content of the children's own letters.

The letters sent by children to their fathers are overwhelmingly concerned with domestic details and family life. This is unsurprising, as it made up almost the entirety of the children's experience, but it is nevertheless significant as it represents a determined effort to keep the father involved in the family unit. Children reported what they had done at school, at the weekend or on holiday, as well as the actions of siblings and other relatives, to keep their fathers up to date about significant happenings and relationships in their lives. By taking an interest and responding with questions or comments on such news, fathers were seeking to participate in the daily lives of their children. If they couldn't be there in person to share in their children's domestic routine, fathers enquired and prompted their children for details that would allow them to imagine the world they were missing. For the children, sharing their adventures with their fathers via a letter and receiving their interest in return meant that their fathers became a part of their memory and understanding of the events and people in their lives.

Fathers, in turn, often wrote to their children in a way that mirrored the domestic detail of life at home. Indeed, much of the day-to-day business of work in the trenches consisted of entirely domestic chores, from cleaning and equipping the trenches to the preparation and serving of meals. Regular soldiers carried out these tasks under the supervision of their officers, whose responsibility it was to ensure all were well catered for. When men were sick or injured it was other men who cared for them, and thus, very much like the women they had left behind, men became immersed in the domestic details of caring for themselves and each other. In *Dismembering the Male* Joanna Bourke has argued that for the men fighting in the trenches 'home remained the touchstone for all their actions' and that men actually pursued domesticity in an attempt 'to regain their sense of honour and a taste of contentment'.[27]

So it was easy for fathers to summon up a domestic image to describe to their children and wrote of living conditions, food, animals and friends in a way designed to give their children a way of picturing their absent father in circumstances they could relate to. Lieutenant E. Hopkinson's letter to his young daughter Mildred, written in December 1916, is a good example of this. Then a 2nd Lieutenant in the 1/8th Battalion Sherwood Foresters, Hopkinson describes the contents of a Christmas parcel received from the civic authorities in Nottingham, writing:

I said I would tell you what the parcel contained. Well here they are:

1 tin plum pudding
1 tin milk
1 tin Dubbin
1 tin peppermints
½ lb Cadbury's chocolate
1 tablet carbolic soap
1 stick shaving soap
1 packet butterscotch
1 pair leather laces
1 carriage candle
1 packet bachelors buttons
1 Christmas card

Now do you not think that is a very useful parcel for me to receive out here. The difference between this years one and last is, a plum pudding is substituted for a plum cake and a packet of butterscotch is put in extra. We have had two plum puddings and they were good. The other things I have not yet sampled.

The rest of Hopkinson's letter contains news of the platoon's sports fixtures and score line and his suggested answers to a spelling game begun by his daughter. In return, Hopkinson poses her a maths question and enquires about school and homework. In response to the news that the family back home have been trying to catch a rat that has taken up residence at the end of the garden, Hopkinson writes:

> Of course out here it is nothing to see scores of rats when in the trenches and in billets. At night when I am in bed I can hear the rats running about in the loft room above. But I do hope you will get rid of them down the garden because they are not at all pleasant companions.

Centring letters home on domestic details was perhaps particularly necessary when the children were very young, when fathers may have feared that an extended absence would be too much for the bond they had had such little time to build up. One such father was A.C. Stanton, who was called up late in 1916 and began service as an Air Mechanic in the 13th Kite Balloon Section of the Royal Flying Corps in February 1917. Stanton's two children, Peggy and Hugh, were just four and three, respectively, when Stanton was sent to the Western Front to carry out meteorological ballooning duties in the summer of 1917. During the war Stanton's wife Dora and the children moved from Wembley to Highgate in North London and the family corresponded regularly, Stanton sending the children 18 letters between April 1917 and December 1918.

In his first letter home to the children Stanton explains: 'When you are both a little more grown up you will know why it was that I had to go away from home for a time and leave you and mother'. But the rest of the letter is nothing but light-hearted. After drawing a picture of a tent and explaining that that is where he now lives, Stanton goes on:

> We got some pretty plants and put them round the tent to make it nice and like home. I expect the plants belonged to some little girl like you Peggy, once, but she had to leave them and go away.

> In the place here there are three little kittens, grey with long hair, fluffy ones, they have a good time. Nearby are woods with ever so many big trees, and little snowdrops grow under the trees, and in the trees are lots of birds called magpies, black and white. Ask mother to tell you about magpies, they are like some little children who chatter all the time and play tricks.

> The other day I saw a soldier who had a monkey for a pet, the monkey sat on the ground and squeaked when I gave him one of the raisins which mother sent me out, he was so pleased to show all his teeth.

You must try and be good children and kind to mother, and when I come home we shall all have a big treat together.

From reading the next few letters Stanton sent to his young children, you could be forgiven for thinking that his portion of the Western Front had more in common with a farmyard or wildlife sanctuary, so full is it with bunny rabbits (which he sketches), goats (which the men feed cake to) and dogs (that he befriends), than a battlefield. But the tactic works, and the children respond (in letters written by their mother, but addressed and signed by them) with enquiries about the animals and a plea to bring one of the dogs home after the war is over.

However, as the fighting continues it appears Stanton is beginning to miss his children more and more, and when he writes to them to wish them both happy birthday in October 1917 he writes:

I should very much like to see you for a little while out here, as there aren't any children here, only big grown-up men, but some day the children will all come back with their mothers and fathers, and the boys and girls will play in the holes and corners where the men have to live now.

I shall tell you more about this when I come home, so until then you must wait for me and be ever so kind to each other and to dear mother, who is taking so much care of you.

From then on the war itself makes more of an entrance into the letters, perhaps as Stanton begins to forget his earlier concern for his children's age, or because he wants to bring them closer to him by giving them a clearer understanding of the life he is living. Hughie is told of the airships and balloons Stanton sees and rides in, while Peggy is told about all the French children in the neighbouring villages and how their lives have been altered by the war. In the summer of 1918 Stanton writes a letter to the children with frightening detail about the war that would have been unthinkable in his first few letters. He writes:

Let me tell you something pretty I saw the other day. You know that where I am the Germans fire great big guns at us and the shot from these guns goes off in the air with a great noise, and then all the pieces of shot come falling down, and sometimes may hurt some-body. Well the other morning I was going down the road when I saw two children a little girl about as big as Margaret and a tiny little boy, not quite so big as Hughie; just as I came up to them a big shot came whistling along, and the little girl at once put her arms round her little brother, and hid his face in her apron until the shot had burst with a great noise and all the pieces had fallen down. They both looked up at me and laughed. Now wasn't that pretty! I hope you will both be as kind and brave as those two little children.

Then, perhaps as an attempt to allay the children's fears, Stanton goes on, in his first and last attempt to explain warfare, to say:

I have to carry a helmet with me to put on when there are pieces of shot falling down. A helmet is a sort of hat made of iron. Years ago before there were any guns Soldiers wore what is called armour, that is pieces of iron over their clothes to prevent them being hurt by swords and spears. The bravest of these soldiers were called knights, and they rode on horses. They went about the country doing all sorts of brave deeds, and generally they found a lovely princess in the end and married her. And although we don't wear armour now-a-days, except the helmet I told you about, there are still lots of brave deeds that can be done, and there are princesses too, but you have to watch for them. I found one once, but perhaps I will tell you about that another time.

Stanton's only method of explaining war to his children is to compare it to the tales of knights and princesses they would be familiar with from their storybooks. By doing this, Stanton escapes with them into a fantasy world where he too can be a knight doing brave deeds for their princess–mother. During the two years that Stanton is away from his family Peggy and Hughie start school, attending Home School, which appears to be a small, independent school with a progressive curriculum, near to their Highgate home. In celebrating this beginning of school life with his children, Stanton obviously wants to give them the same kind of encouragement as he would have done had he been at home, but missing such a milestone in his children's lives was clearly a wrench to Stanton:

Mother told me in her letter about your going to school and about all the wonderful things you are beginning to do there. I hope that whatever you do whether it is singing or painting or feeding the birds, that you will always try to do it as well as you possibly can, and you will find that whatever it is will become easier and better all the time.

Always ask questions when you want to know about anything, but be sure to try and listen to what the answer is, then you won't have to learn the same thing over and over again, but before asking any questions have a little 'think' and see if you can find out yourself what you want to know, then ask and see if you were right.

Other fathers also took an active interest in their children's education despite being separated from them by the war. In the huge collection of over 100 letters written by the four Butling children to their father Private A.J. Butling, serving in France with the Army Service Corps, and his letters to them, there are constant references to school and regular updates on all exams and marks received. When the first of the letters were sent in 1916 the eldest child, George, was 13, Eric was 11, Grace 7 and Ben just 2 years old. The family lived in Wavertree, Liverpool, and both George and Eric wrote almost weekly to their father; he in turn wrote regularly to them, sometimes just one letter which was to be read to the others, sometimes individually. In his first letter to his father, sent in March 1916, George is obviously well up on events of the war and keen to show his father how well he is doing at school, writing:

Just a few lines to let you know I am still thinking of you in the present grave crisis but I think that in the next few days the tide will turn; anyhow we must wait and see what happens. I see that the Germans have captured quite a number of tanks and guns but I expect you will know more about that than us in Blighty.

There is a vigorous offensive in our school this last week – as the exams are on, but I think that I have done fine in the majority so far especially arith. Geometry, nature study, and not so bad in Latin and algebra but I had better not say too much as we have not finished yet.

The war was on the boys' minds often at school, with George suggesting 'A First Class Naval Battle' as the subject for a drawing lesson and Eric drawing a machine gun for his handwork exam. But they were not distracted in their work, with George especially regularly coming top in his class for some of his subjects and being rewarded at Christmas 1916 with a day's holiday for each subject in which he excelled. Writing excitedly to his father, George said:

We are to have as many holidays as we are top in, and we can choose which day we like, so when you come home on leave I shall have my odd days, so let me know in time so that I can apply for them.

Christmas 1916 was also an exciting time for seven-year-old Grace, who wrote to her father of a visit into town to see Father Christmas:

> I went to the Grotto with Mother and Ben and Mrs Himman and Willie came with us. I was very glad when I saw what I got, there was a tank there, and soldiers peeping up out of the trenches to see if the Germans were coming. My present was a slate and when I got home I began to draw on it.

The war came even closer to the children's lives at home when, in February 1918, the boys got a new teacher at school, a discharged soldier Eric described as 'a fine chap'. This fired the boys' imagination, and Eric wrote to his father all about the new teacher's description of trench warfare and how the guns were disguised: 'he told us of one gun which was disguised so well that it was there fifteen months without being found out'. A month later George reported an excursion to see some of the weapons of war:

> Last night an illuminated tramcar in the form of a tank came down Smithdown Rd so we all went to see it. The tractors were edged with electric light and at various other parts, altogether making a fine show, also a dreadnought was towed on behind looking very grotesque as it was all in darkness.

When Private Butling wrote to his children, his letters contained a mixture of domestic detail, entreaties to good behaviour and comments about the war, in differing amounts perhaps depending on the age of the child the letter was addressed to. To seven-year-old Grace, Butling made light of his domestic situation, attempting to make his sleeping quarters sound like somewhere his daughter might like to play:

> I am writing it [letter] in my bunk on the box that mother sent the cakes in. You and Benny would call it a cubby house if you saw it and want to play in it, I expect, wouldn't it be fun. One man sleeps underneath me and another man above me. The top man has to go up a ladder to his bunk which is level with the eighth step of the ladder. Mine is on the fourth. So you see we have to do a little gymnastics when we go to bed.

But when he writes to the older Eric this cubby house has lost some of its charm:

I shall soon be getting in to bed beg pardon, my bunk (a sort of cubby house) with two blankets, waterproof sheet and my overcoat. Fancy it? Guess not. Much love etc, Yours Dad.

Although the letters were addressed to a particular boy, Private Butling always intended George and Eric to share them, and, as well as encouraging them in their school work, he also took seriously his responsibilities as an absent father for their moral upbringing. Unable to be there in person to show and teach them to be conscientious, honourable boys, Butling sometimes wrote serious letters, advising them of their responsibilities while he was away and entreating them to behave. In April 1917 he wrote to Eric:

I should very much like to be with you for a few evenings, or, for good, but there is a great amount of work for us to do here yet so don't expect me yet a while.

Well Eric my lad, *I am expecting both you and George to be honourable boys and I wish you both to grow up thorough Christian children. It is up to you both* and I hope you will always remember that whatever scrapes you get in to.

But it was to the eldest, George, that Butling wrote in most detail of his feelings about the war. Replying to a letter from George asking when he will get some home leave, Butling writes:

At present I cannot tell when that will be as since this 'Push' has started it has altered things somewhat. The Kaiser wishing to annihilate us, especially us British, evidently they still treat us with contempt. I take off my hat to our fallen comrades deeply deploring their loss, at the same time greatly admiring their noble sacrifice and valiant stand against such enormous odds.

It is a revelation that, once more the British spirit still lives that has been handed down to us to take up and carry on.

The war took its toll on Private Butling, and it appears that it was George who was most sensitive to his father's state of mind. In a comment which suggests Private Butling may have been suffering from some of the symptoms of shell shock, George wrote in September 1918:

I am glad to hear that you have got over your toothache, and I hope that you will remain free from all complaints in the future, including 'night alarms' and such like.

Despite surviving the war itself, Private Butling died of dysentery in 1919 after serving in France for three years.

It is clear from many of the letters how preoccupied some fathers were with the differences they would see in their children when they returned home. Realising that they were likely to be away from home for years rather than months, the men who were called up from 1916 did not expect the war to end quickly. Those with young children knew that when they returned their sons and daughters would have developed both physically and mentally while they were away. As we have seen, many fathers took a keen interest in their children's schooling, but for fathers whose children were too young for school it was the physical changes that preyed on their minds. When Sapper Ernest Williams was called up into the Royal Engineers in 1916 his two children, Marjorie and Harold, were too young to go to school. The letters he writes have to be read to the children by their mother, and the ones they send to him are penned by her and illustrated by the children. To begin with, he addresses these letters to 'My dear little Marjorie' and 'My dear sonny Harold', but by the following year, after Marjorie has turned five, he is acknowledging her growth, beginning 'My dear little (I mean big) pet Marjorie'. In that letter of April 1917 he goes on:

> Mother tells me that you are growing so big she has to make 2 new dresses for you – never mind how big you grow I will put you on my shoulders when I come home – because I am getting such a strong daddy.

All of Williams' letters to his children are of a purely family nature; he rarely mentions the war at all, and seems to dwell on things they have done together in the past and what they might do as a family in the future. He clearly misses his wife and children desperately and is keen to remind them of his love and encourage their bond with him despite their separation. On many occasions he write notes to Harold, who I think was perhaps a year or two older than Marjorie, chastising him for not writing to him, saying things like:

> Harold dear every letter mother sends you *must* send me a note in it every time. Don't forget that your daddy wants a note from his big boy every time.

While training at Hitchin in Hertfordshire, Williams wrote to Marjorie of an incident which illustrates how often his children were on his mind:

Well yesterday I saw a big bear in the street and the man told him to dance and when the man started singing – the bear danced – oh it was funny and all the children did enjoy themselves. I asked one little girl if her name was Marjorie and she said no it is Maggie. You see she looked something like you so I just wondered if her name was the same as yours.

Although none of the children's letters to their father survive, it is clear from comments about them in his letters that Marjorie in particular was a regular correspondent. She sent him pictures she had drawn, which he displayed on the wall near his bunk, and sent him flowers. She also wrote to him of the new clothes she had been given and told him jokes and stories about what she had been doing. At one point in 1917, while he was training at Newark, the family came to stay nearby, and it is obvious from his letters that a great deal of thought and planning on his part went in to where his wife and children were to stay and what they might do while they were there. To all intents and purposes, the Williams family were trying to maintain their family unit in the face of such a long separation, and letters became the chief means for them to develop this relationship.

By May 1918, when Williams writes to Marjorie on the occasion of her seventh birthday, he has been away since she was four years old. He has missed almost half of her life, but, although tinged with sorrow, his letter is filled with affection:

My darling sweet pet own girlie Marjorie,

Your daddy sends to his darling daughter, a special letter all by itself to wish her very many happy returns of her birthday. Fancy she is 7 years old – she must be getting a big girlie now and I must not say little girlie any more, but if she grows as big as a house she will always be her Daddy's own loved girlie. Oh daddy is going to try so hard to get this silly old war finished so that he can get back home again and be with his girlie every day and not to be miles and miles away from her over the sea. I do hope you have a jolly day – that it is fine sunshine and that you have a good time all the time. I should like to send you a box of lovely flowers but the poor things would be all withered away before you could get them so I will let them go on growing in the fields and gardens and just imagine that you can smell them.

Ta ta my darling pet. God bless and take care of you and dear loving brother Harold and that sweetest of all, our Mother. Heaps and heaps of love and kisses from your own always loving Daddy.

Williams and many other fathers included sketches in their letters. Sometimes these were of animals or trains or flowers, things they thought their children would enjoy. Other times the men sketched their surroundings, showing their children their uniform or sleeping arrangements. Williams drew animals and cartoon sketches designed to amuse his children, while the poet E.G. Buckeridge illustrated his journey to France for his young son Anthony. Beside a detailed picture of a boat Buckeridge wrote:

I suppose you are now *quite* the man of the house now that I am away, even though you are only 4 ½ years old. This is Daddy going over in the steamer to France. I hope you can see him. He is the important looking gentleman in the bows. There wasn't room to draw the captain and the crew. I expect they are somewhere downstairs don't you. This is Daddy in his new tin bonnet. He is somewhere inside.

By illustrating their letters, most often to quite young children, these fathers are helping to create the story of their war experience in the minds of their children. Just like in the picture books they have at home, these fathers are appearing as characters in their own life story. For children as young as four-year-old Anthony Buckeridge or the Williams children, imagining their absent father in circumstances so unlike any they had ever experienced must have been almost impossible. Their fathers, realising that their children would be confused and troubled by their absence, create and illustrate a story for them. They are the hero, embarking on an adventure, crossing the sea aboard a steamer and making a home for themselves in strange and exciting tunnels. The children in turn could use these illustrations, just as they did with their picture books, to become enthralled by the tale of their father's adventure.

To begin with, fathers and their children looked for common experiences, details of domestic life that they could share with each other. They turned to the familiar, to animals and plants and food and surroundings in an attempt to keep up a mutual connection. But as the war went on, and the gaps between their meetings lengthened, fathers had to look for some other way to forge an identification with their children. It was no longer enough to rely on shared experiences, especially when very young children perhaps could not even really remember what it was like to have their father at home at all. Instead, some fathers attempted to create a new reality for their children through their letters. These fathers became characters in a narrative of the war, pictures on a page or heroes in a partially invented landscape. They told their children the truth about the more pleasant aspects of their surroundings and then fictionalised the rest to produce a tale that was both positive and exciting. Children in their turn responded to these letters with interest; they wanted to play with the dogs their fathers had met and sleep in the cubby house bunks where their dads went to bed. They wrote regularly, often with immense detail, about what had gone on at school, the marks they had received, the friends they had seen and the food they had eaten, maintaining the bonds with this central figure in their emotional life who for the present could not be with them.

War news

Not all fathers kept the war from their children; some discussed it at length, describing every aspect of their life at the Front. In most cases these letters are addressed to older children, perhaps because fathers believed that the children were already well aware of the war and what it entailed. Letters describing the war range in style from jokey, gung-ho references to serious, descriptive passages which show that not all parents were at pains to hide the war from their children.

Captain J. Foulis of the Queen's Own Cameron Highlanders clearly felt his young niece Nancy should be instilled with a strong sense of the purpose behind the fighting, and wrote to her regularly after he joined up in 1914. His letters are funny and brutal at the same time, suggesting that he knew that his niece would share in his ghoulish delight in fighting the Germans. The first one sent in October 1914 is short, simply saying:

> Thank you very much for your letter which I got today. It was very wicked of these bad Germans to shoot Uncle Willie, so I hope to get near them soon and shoot a great lot of them just the way that Uncle Teddy shoots the bunnies. We are kept very busy here marching and practising shooting so as to be very good at killing the Kaiser when we go to Germany.

A year later he has more detail to give about life in the army, and, although playing down the danger he is in, still describes a far more gruesome war than many of the other adults who write to children from the trenches:

> I have now got over here and am living in a trench close to the Germans. It is rather a jolly trench for there are all sorts of little houses and snug little holes and corners dug out everywhere. Some of these little houses we use for sleeping in and other for our meals.
>
> The 'Germs' are about 100 yards away, and we often throw shells and bombs and things at each other, but our trench is a jolly strong one so that they cannot do us any harm.
>
> We have got a lot of enormous rats and tiny mice. They scuttle and scamper about everywhere and do not bother about the war at all.
>
> This morning one of our soldiers killed a large rat with a spade. Now we have a bomb throwing machine, so we put this rat onto the machine and threw it all the way into the German trench. I wonder if they had it for breakfast?
>
> It is rather pretty at night here there are so many wonderful lights in the sky. You see the flashing of big guns and of bursting shells very often, but mostly a long way off. Then there are the rockets which are sent up every few minutes both by ourselves and the Germans. They light the sky almost like daylight, so that you can see every blade of grass in the ground between us and the Boches. They are fine to watch.

Foulis seems confident that his niece will appreciate the humour in the rat throwing incident as much as he and his men evidently did, suggesting that he remembers very well the fun children can get out of the truly disgusting. As an officer, Foulis was trusted to censor his own mail, and, although he refers to killing Germans in his first letter, he plays down any suggestion that he himself is in danger. Perhaps conscious of Nancy's age, or perhaps reluctant to admit the truth to himself, Foulis describes an exciting, amusing war – much like a game his niece might enjoy.

Other men who enlisted at the start of the war also seem keen to share their experiences with their children. R.P. Harker was in his thirties when he enlisted as a regular soldier after failing to secure a commission at the very start of the war. He appears to have been a widower with a 13-year-old son, Freddie, at boarding school. Harker's letters to Freddie are full of the details of army life, in fact containing almost nothing else, and at times he sounds more like a school boy than the one he is writing to. He shows a ready acceptance of the hardships of army life and a keen sense of patriotism, which he appears to have wanted to pass on to his son. In November 1914 he wrote to Freddie describing the men's attitude to fighting:

> Many thanks for your last letter. Awfully glad to hear that you beat Bigshotte so easily, and so glad you were up one in the form that week. The sketch of the destroyer with the gun on it is quite good on your last letter. We are billeted in a school here and this town is filled with soldiers. Our army seem to be doing magnificently and our soldiers don't think much of the Germans as fighting men, but the German artillery is awfully good and also their machine guns, without them they would have made a poor show. They have all sorts of unsportsmanlike tricks and attack our men disguised in khaki and sometimes kilts and shout out sentences in English saying 'don't shoot, we are so-and-so', giving the name of some English regiment. They also shout out 'cease fire' in English and give our signals. I don't think the war will be over before next spring at the earliest.

Harker was clearly revelling in his new role as a soldier. So keen was he to get out to France that he had enlisted as a regular soldier despite the fact that he would have undoubtedly got a commission had he waited a couple of months. Harker, almost certainly the product of a public school education himself, writes very much in the style Paul Fussell has termed British Phlegm. 'The trick here is to affect to be entirely unflappable; one speaks as if the war were entirely normal and matter-of-fact'.[28] Harker's letters are breezy and confident and he embraces Army life to the full. In many ways his letters are reminiscent of boys' adventure fiction, popular at the time and discussed in the next chapter, fiction Freddie was likely to be reading at school. All is exciting, the British are upstanding, fine chaps, while the Germans are underhand and sneaky. By depicting the war as a great adventure and by presenting himself as the hero of the tale to his teenage son, Harker is helping to reconcile Freddie to his absence while boosting his own sense of pride and confidence.

Shortly after being commissioned into the North Staffordshire Regiment in March 1915, Harker was killed by sniper fire. In the following months his sister Ethel corresponded with an old family friend and fellow soldier. From one letter it is clear that Ethel feels that Freddie has not been too affected by his father's death:

> It is a merciful thing that Freddie does not realise things but all the same it seems inexpressibly sad that it should be so after Robert having for years past given up such a lot that Freddie might have everything.

It is clear, however, from autobiographical accounts of public boarding school life during wartime that Freddie may well have felt his father's death acutely but been afraid to show his feelings. As the intention of the British public schools at this time was to educate future British gentlemen, it was important that the children educated in them were able to control their feelings and handle whatever misfortune befell them. As such, the children were not encouraged to display emotions that might be construed as a sign of weakness; instead, they were expected to put on a brave face and cope with their grief alone. The war, in most of these schools' eyes, was a necessary evil and one that should be supported wholeheartedly. The schools were proud of their old boys in uniform, and children were expected to be equally proud of their fathers and brothers for defending the empire.

In *Exhumation* Christopher Isherwood talks of how the boys at his prep school had what he refers to as a cult of the dead:

> Several boys, including myself, had lost their fathers; many of us had lost a near relative. It is untrue to say that we were callous; I think we mourned in our own barely conscious way. But the concept of Grief, as practiced by adults, was almost meaningless to us. We could only understand it in terms of drama, over which we gloated, and of social prestige, which commanded our sincere respect.[29]

Isherwood also remembers that, when a boy was called out in the middle of a lesson to be told that a father or brother had been killed, the standard response of his friends, when he finally returned, would be to ask 'did you blub much?' Following the death of a relative, boys wore black crepe armbands 'with grave pride' and this brought with it the privilege of not being 'ragged' by the other boys.[30]

> On one occasion during a friendly, laughing scuffle, a boy's armband got torn. Immediately he burst into tears of indignation, crying, 'look what you've done, you swine!' and we let go of him at once, equally shocked at this violation of taboo.[31]

Perhaps most upsettingly, Isherwood recounts the story of a boy who pretended to the others that his father was dead.

> He was unpopular and lonely, and I suppose he was desperate for some recognition.[32]

The boys discovered his lie and subjected him to what was in their system of justice the equivalent of capital punishment – they threw him into a gorse bush. This suggests that the prestige associated with losing a father was sufficiently great to elevate an unpopular and clearly very unhappy boy to a level that would demand, if not the friendship, then at least the respect of his schoolfellows. Equally, this status was revered and respected by the boys, and anyone abusing it was dealt with brutally.

It was not only to boys that fathers sometimes felt comfortable describing the more frightening aspects of the war in their letters. British-born Canadian Captain Ivan Finn of the tenth Battalion CEF wrote to his daughter living in England in 1915 about the conditions he was living in:

> My darling Margaret
>
> Father sends his love to you. I cannot write very much because there is such a fearful noise from our guns. I hope that I shall see you soon again and that the war will end quickly. A lot of farms are burning up and the sun is very bright and warm.
>
> I live in a hole and feel very dirty for I have been unable to wash since I left England. The other day I saw a battle in front where the poison gases were used. It looked like a horrible green yellow curtain hanging from the sky.
>
> Now my darling I will end. God bless you and keep you always.
>
> Your loving father, Ivan.

Whether Margaret was alarmed by this or not it is impossible to know. The effects of poison gas were known by the public at this time and wounded soldiers were a common sight in England, but Captain Finn obviously believed his daughter would be more interested than scared by his descriptions. For some fathers the need to share what they were seeing was overwhelming and far outweighed their concerns for what their children might need to hear. In a fascinating letter that avoided the censor, Private W. Vernon serving on the Western Front wrote to his daughter Lucy of the Allied retreat from the Marne after the German advance in the spring of 1918. Vernon's wife was illiterate, and so it was through Lucy that husband and wife communicated throughout the war. The first half of the letter is fairly predictable, dealing with the weather and family matters, much like the hundreds of other letters fathers had been writing to their children. But then the second half of the letter explodes after Vernon adds pages to his unsealed letter that has already been passed by the censor. He begins by telling Lucy about where he has been and how and where he was injured and recovered. Then he begins to talk of the retreat:

> You should have seen us retreating, the roads were packed with troops and horses, guns, limbers, Red Cross Ambulances, French and ours and wounded walking for miles and miles. They daren't stop for fear of Jerry catching them but the worst of all was the civilians, they had to run for their lives and leave everything they had, only just what they stood up in and plenty we saw with a little baby in a pram and a few odd things, just what they could lay hold of and they were on the road for days and days sleeping on the roadside at night, it was heartbreaking to see them. Some of our A.S.C. drivers would give them a lift on the wagons.

> While we were retreating Jerry was over the top of us with his aeroplanes dropping bombs and firing his machine gun at us and we started firing at them. We brought one down with our rifles. It was fine sport.

Again we hear the echoes of adventure fiction in the 'fine sport' of bringing down an enemy aircraft. Or is the final phrase an example of Private Vernon adopting the enthusiastic language his officers used to inspire their men? Then again, it is possible that Vernon took a genuine delight in shooting down the plane. After all, perhaps Vernon had just spent several years living in trenches, being shot at by Germans, and so felt justified in revelling in his enemy's death. Joanna Bourke has explored the often ambivalent feelings soldiers have towards their victims, noting that 'although the act of killing another person in battle may invoke a wave of nauseous distress, it may also incite intense feelings of pleasure'.[33] Bourke has described how successfully hitting the enemy gave men a sense of their own power and that adding another 'kill' to their score was often a cause of much celebration. Importantly, however, Bourke also recognises the link between fantasy and experience. As martial combat has become an integral part of the modern imagination through literature and films, so soldiers have gone to war already excited by the possibility of killing. As we shall see, late nineteenth-century children's literature was full of tales of imperial battles and military adventures, and so First World War soldiers had an image of warfare in their minds well before they arrived on the Western Front. According to Bourke, in the act of killing fantasy and experience are intertwined, and must remain so for the sake of the soldier's moral survival. By imbuing their actions with a level of fantasy, borrowed from literature or films, 'combatants [are] able to construct a story around acts of exceptional violence which could render their actions pleasurable'.[34]

Here again we see the idea that men, in describing their experiences to their children in this way, were casting themselves as the heroes of a story their children might enjoy. By linking their own fantasies about the war they were fighting with the ones their children read in adventure fiction, these soldiers were attempting to find a place for the war within a fantasy world they both understood. Children could imagine their fathers in a tale that always had a happy ending, while fathers could reconcile their actions to themselves by locating them in the familiar language of their own childhood stories. Perhaps because they were writing to children, men like Foulis and Vernon felt freer to employ this language of fantasy. In Vernon's case there is a stark contrast between his description of the German advance and his account of the shooting down of the plane. At first he pours his heart out to his daughter about the realities of warfare, detailing the 'heartbreaking' sight of the civilian refugees fleeing their homes. But then he returns to the language of adventure stories when he describes his own part in killing a man. Clearly Vernon was not insensitive to human suffering; he just chose to set his own act of violence in a different light.

Vernon is well aware of the risk he is taking in sending this letter, but it appears he just cannot stop himself now he has the chance for the first time to tell his family what the war is really like:

> Dear Lucy, don't tell anybody what I have told you in this letter for if I was to get found out I should get Court Martialled. I could fill 20 or 30 pages if I liked telling you my experiences, it seems quite different writing when you can put what you like in the letter without anyone censoring it after you.
>
> This is the first time I have had a chance to send a few exciting lines.

I think I will now draw to a close. You will wonder what I have been doing sending such a long letter, so with love to all,

From your Loving Father xxxxxx

Good Night

The last part about how different writing a letter is without having to worry about the censor may explain the lack of detail and concentration on family matters in many of the other men's letters home. For Vernon, it was the possibility of telling the truth to his daughter that caused him to write in such an eager and detailed way. The difference between the first half, read by the censor, and the second is telling. A bland and uninteresting letter written by a man who appears slightly bored and perhaps only writing to his child out of duty becomes an exciting and moving letter when Vernon is free to write as he likes. He risked court martial and possible imprisonment for sending this letter, but was clearly desperate to share with his family what he was experiencing.

Some fathers would never see an end to the war. Lying in a Voluntary Aid Detachment (VAD) hospital in Earls Colne, Essex, Sergeant F.H. Gautier of the 11th Battalion, Cheshire Regiment, knew he was dying. From there he wrote to his young daughter Marie with a note on the front of the envelope saying 'To my dear daughter Marie when she is able to understand'. The Gautiers' eldest son, Albert, had recently been killed at Ypres, and in this letter Gautier is calling on his daughter to remember him and her brother, whom he knows she will be too young to remember:

To my darling daughter Marie,

Dearly loved daughter this my letter to you is written in grief. I had hoped to spend many happy years with you after the war was over and to see you grow up into a good and happy woman. I am writing because I want you in after years to know how dearly I loved you, I know that you are too young to keep me in your memory. I know your dear mother will grieve. Be a comfort to her, remember when you are old enough that she lost her dear brave son, your brother, and me, your father, within a short time. Your brother was a dear brave boy, honour his memory for he loved you and your brothers dearly and he died like a brave soldier in defence of his home and Country. May God guide and keep you safe and that at last we may all meet together in his eternal rest. I am your loving and affectionate father

F. H. Gautier xxxxxxxxxxxxxxxxxxxxxxxxxxxxxxxxxxxxxxxxxxxxxxxxxxxxx

Gautier died, two months after writing this letter, in June 1916. Marie treasured the letter, keeping it with a postcard from her brother Albert which said 'I shall come home to see you some day, love brother Albert'. Here Gautier is using the letter form to communicate with his youngest child over a space in time rather than a physical space, which was the case with most letters written by fathers to their children. It lets him address his child in a manner not appropriate to her age at the time and allows him to appeal to her to support her mother and remember him and her brother in a way a baby never could.

Some men seem to have had no hesitation in telling their children about the realities of trench fighting. They are either matter-of-fact about it, like Harker or Captain Finn, or they appear to revel in it, like Foulis or Vernon. It is interesting to note that all but one of these letters describing war news was sent to girls. This suggests that the men recognised the childish interest their daughters and nieces would have in the ghoulish detail of battle and did not believe they would be upset by what they heard. By describing scenes of firing rats at the Germans or shooting down aircraft with rifles, these men are likening their experience to childhood fun – they are merely taking part in an adventurous game rather than in a dangerous war. They did this to reassure their children, but also perhaps to convince themselves that what they were seeing and doing was nothing more than the sort of thing they would have loved to do as children.

Conclusion

Writing to their children gave men a chance to return to the themes of play and adventure that had sustained their pre-war understanding of warfare. Through their words and illustrations men constructed a wartime identity for themselves which they presented to their children. This creation of a soldier–father, who lived in holes in the ground and who saw danger but was never threatened by it, allowed both children and fathers themselves to come to terms with what they were facing. Children could feel positive about their fathers' absence because their fathers were positive themselves. In return, fathers could be reconciled to their new role as potential killers by recalling the language of fantasy that had first brought warfare to their attention.

Michael Roper has suggested that the circumstances of trench life led young men, and particularly junior officers, to identify with their own mothers as they fulfilled a maternal role caring for the men under their command. When they organised or undertook the provision of food, clothing or nursing duties they were performing the very tasks their own mothers had once performed for them.[35] If, as Roper suggests, this gave them a closer understanding and identification with their own mothers, is it not also possible that it led married men to identify with their wives in their duty of performing the maternal role for their own children? Did fathers have a new understanding of what it meant to care for the physical and mental well being of their children? The concerns over health and adequate diet expressed by many fathers in their letters to their children certainly suggest that they now recognised the fundamental importance of these issues.

If caring for other men did lead fathers to identify with their wives as mothers, and thus see their role as parents more clearly, perhaps it is also possible that as soldiers, with no control over their own fate, they may also have identified with their children. Powerless to decide on their own actions, the experience of fighting during the First World War has been described as emasculating. But does this experience not also have much in common with being a child? Children had little or no control over their own lives in Edwardian England and were dependent on their parents for their material well being. So perhaps their fathers, in a similar situation, gained a new insight into their children's position and felt closer to them as a result.

Most of these letters suggest close family relationships in which families were attempting to maintain and strengthen their bonds by writing to each other. They bridged a physical separation as well as a vast gap in their experience of the war by telling each other about what they were doing, and also what they were missing in not being together. Each side came to rely on letters as a sign of the continuing existence of love from the other as well as proof of their health and life. Fathers parented from a distance, backing up their wives and providing their children with a link to the world outside the domestic sphere. Children learnt about the war through the separation from their fathers as much as through any descriptions of the war itself that their fathers might give them. The war meant grief and separation for millions of homes throughout Britain, and even children whose fathers did return in the end had already experienced the loss of years of family life.

3
War Imagined

Introduction

C.H. Rolph played with his friends in the streets of Fulham during the war. He was 12 years old when war broke out and remembers:

> The percussion cap pistols came out again, old walking sticks were converted to dummy rifles, and the Prussophobia of the past ten years became so universal among my street urchin comrades that no one along the whole road wanted to be a German and it was difficult to arrange battles.[1]

Rolph believes he was more aware of current affairs than other children his age as he was learning shorthand with his father and would take down newspaper stories read aloud by his mother. He remembers that the toys and games of his childhood were often associated with the events of the world around them. In the years leading up to the war he says:

> Warlike weapons had begun appearing in the toy-shop windows and, in due course, in the streets. The Sidney Street siege of 1911 had aroused interest in that deadly and haphazard little firework, the Mauser automatic pistol... Imitation Mausers appeared as 'spring guns' with a tiny spring operated plunger for ejecting small marbles, ball-bearings or pebbles, and they appeared too as pocket torches and water pistols.[2]

Using toys, games, fiction and magazines, produced by adults but consumed by children, we can attempt to understand how adult preoccupations and desires to influence children's understanding of the war were appropriated by the children themselves to inform their play and shape their interpretation of the war. Toy production and juvenile literature show us both what images adults wanted children to have about the war and also what they felt children would enjoy. Motivated by commercial concerns, toy makers and publishers were aware of what would sell and attempted to both shape the market and respond to children's desires. Editorials in the trade press make it clear that manufacturers knew that children's play and imaginations were being fired by the war and so sought to produce products that would appeal to their market. In turn these products fostered children's imagination, providing details and props to support their existing imaginative narratives.

Children adopted the war as a recurring theme in their games because they were surrounded by it in everyday life. Most had a personal connection with fathers or brothers in the armed forces, and, as we shall consider in subsequent chapters, children learnt about the war at school, and many participated in the war effort through uniformed youth groups. What is harder to discover is how the war entered children's imagination, what place it had in their games and how important war play was in shaping their understanding of the real war, or their sense of themselves. Did playing at soldiers or nurses make children want to be soldiers and nurses? Did games give children an opportunity to confront fears about absent fathers and brothers? Did children use the war-themed toys they were given in the way that was intended, or did they subvert their use for something else? All this is very difficult to know because of the essentially private way in which children play. Children's games need not have any rules or structure; they can be invented on the spot and can change in purpose or meaning in an instant. Some autobiographers have recorded how they played and what they read, but many have not. From the evidence we do have, it appears that the war entered children's games regardless of whether they had any commercially produced products available to prompt them. Children played games and read books as a way of expressing their own understanding of the war, giving them a chance to identify with their absent fathers and brothers.

The toy industry in Britain had benefited from the consumer boom of the 1870s and onwards. Technological advances and the reduction of transport costs created a highly competitive manufacturing environment which drove down prices. At the same time, a fall in the cost of food brought on by the opening up of major agricultural resources in

North America and parts of the Empire meant that, allowing for unemployment, average real wages rose by more than 75 per cent between 1867 and 1900. Although this rate of growth decreased during the Edwardian period, wages were still much higher in 1914 than they had been in the late Victorian period. This meant that as families saw their household incomes rise there was more money left over to spend on what might previously have been considered luxuries for their children.[3]

But there were still great variations in the types of toys that might be bought for different children. At the lower end of the social scale, poorer parents might pick up penny toys for their children from the itinerant workers walking the streets of Britain. For more complicated manufactured toys, however, street selling was on the decline. Replacing hawkers were specialised toy shops and department stores, and even stationers, newsagents and post offices had all begun to stock children's gifts. In such shops parents might buy anything from the better-quality dolls and toy soldiers not available on the streets to mechanical toys, toy trains and the popular new construction toys.

Despite this positive expansion in trade, the toy industry was a cause for tension in the immediate pre-war years, as it became part of the trade war with Germany that so terrified the Edwardians. The Germans had a far more established industry than Britain's and produced, on the whole, superior products. The value of German toy imports to Britain had risen from just £45,000 in 1855 to £800,000 by 1900. By the last full year of peace it had reached almost £1,200,000.[4] There are problems in trying to compare this with British production, as the low figures cited in the industry's 1907 Census of Production were called into question at the time and have been rejected since. Kenneth Brown, in his history of the British toy business, has estimated that on the eve of war a figure of £1,000,000 would be plausible.[5] This is considerably less than that of the German imports, but certainly healthy enough to survive and capitalise on the absence of the Germans from the market after hostilities were declared.

Children's play

There is a limited literature on the history of children's toys and games in Britain, and what there is shows little interest in how these objects fit in to the myriad of cultural influences that shaped children's lives in any period in history. There was a plethora of military and war-themed toys, aimed primarily at young boys, available in the British market in the years leading up to and during the First World War. Most histories of children's toys take the view that war toys in any market are simply a reflection of boys' innate interest in aggressive play and all things military. Leslie Daiken, in *Children's Toys Throughout the Ages*, argues, for instance, that: 'If the doll is the universal plaything for a girl, so is the toy soldier the natural toy for boys'. War games, Daiken claims, are simply the expression of the 'herd instinct' in boys of a certain age and are 'merely a variation of the animal hunt'.[6] Boys' response to war games and toy soldiers is instinctive, he believes, and they know what to do and how to play because their response comes from their inherent or natural masculinity. The assumption is that men have always had to 'fight' and 'hunt' in order to survive, and fighting, therefore, has gradually become their natural response to the world. As children, boys act out their natural impulses in play, and so toy soldiers are the obvious choice of toy because they suggest the possibility of battle and conquest.

Antonia Fraser in her *History of Toys* argues similarly that 'it is inevitable that an age which has known wars should produce soldiers and war toys'.[7] For Fraser what is natural is the desire to imitate. Children want to copy their parents, and so they absorb whatever the predominating theme of speech, dress or action happens to be. Significantly, Fraser believes that the popularity of toy soldiers is 'obviously the natural development of an age when a child's admired father is dressed up as G. I. Joe. As long as men go to war and armies exist children will want to play with soldiers'.[8] During the First World War, millions of British fathers were dressed up as our equivalent of G. I. Joe. If Fraser is correct, this would mean that the huge quantity and variety of children's war-themed toys on the market at that time could have been a response to the commercial demand of children to copy the dress and action of their fathers and brothers.

Graham Dawson's *Soldier Heroes* takes issue with this interpretation, however, believing that children's private fantasies are shaped in more subtle ways. He agrees that children can be inspired by events in the world around them to want to act them out for themselves. Thus, toys that mimic or depict currently popular people or events are coveted by children, who want them to enhance their re-enactments in play. In this way the wider social and cultural context can ' "inform" private fantasies and determine the imaginative resonance of particular forms of toy'.[9] But, Dawson believes, children's imaginative investments in particular toys are not wholly dictated by the influences of society and toy makers. Boys' appropriation of wider themes of conflict and adventure 'depends upon an active choice and involves an element of active cultural production by boys themselves, in what can still usefully be called their own "private" imaginings'.[10] Toy makers might direct that a toy is used in a certain way and for a certain purpose, but it is the children themselves who actually determine the place of that toy in their games. Similarly, as we shall see in this chapter, children don't necessarily need any commercially produced toys to play games either based on real events or invented entirely.

But why does it matter what children play with? To answer this question, it is useful to have some understanding of the place of play in the psychic life of the child. Psychoanalysts practising during the war years and into the 1920s and 1930s developed the use of play when working with children, as it allows children to express feelings they are not necessarily able to articulate in words. Melanie Klein, pioneer of the 'play technique', argued that:

> Play for the child is not 'just play'. It is also work. It is not only a way of exploring and mastering the external world but also, through expressing and working through phantasies, a means of exploring and mastering anxieties. In his [sic] play the child dramatizes his phantasies, and in doing so elaborates and works through his conflicts.[11]

Through play, Klein argued, children expressed psychic conflict brought on by anxieties experienced in their relationships with others. In their play these anxieties were given symbolic form, which allowed the children to work through their conflict to the resolution which represented the fulfilment of their unconscious wish. This gave the child pleasure while protecting him/her from the anxiety that would accompany the fulfilment of that wish in real life.

For D.W. Winnicott, a contemporary of Klein's who also worked with children from the 1920s, this place of play is neither the child's inner psychic reality, nor is it part of the external world around them. Rather, it is a between place where children can 'gather objects or phenomenon from external reality and use these in the service of some sample derived from inner or personal reality'.[12] For Winnicott this potential space between the child's inner reality and the external reality of the world around them is where a person's capacity for cultural experience is located. He believes 'cultural experience begins with creative living first manifested in play'.[13]

In order for the analyst to correctly use the 'play technique', Klein insisted that the toys used with the children be 'neutral' in order that their form did not suggest a particular theme of play to the child that might interfere with the expression of their unconscious fantasy. She insisted that 'the human figures, varying only in colour and size, should not indicate any particular occupation'. Klein was thus attempting to take away the importance of any outside cultural influences on the themes of children's play and consequently on the make up of their psychic life.

Drawing on this technique but abandoning the emphasis on neutral toys, Dawson has attempted to understand the ways in which his own childhood passion for war toys unconsciously helped to shape his understanding of his own developing masculinity. Dawson explores the development of his childhood sense of self, through his imaginative investment in, and boyhood fantasies of, adventure and war. He suggests a complicated link between manufactured toys, children's imaginative use of them and their creative development of their sense of self that takes into account the wider social and cultural context of their lives. This has relevance for the millions of British children, and boys in particular, who grew up before and during the war, surrounded by war toys.

If a child's sense of self is in part developed through play, as British psychoanalysts were discovering in the inter-war decades, and can be specifically informed by particular types of toy, as Dawson's self-analysis indicates, then the preponderance of war-themed toys during the First World War helped to shape the identities of those children who grew up playing with them. The existence of so many gendered, military-inspired toys on the market in Britain during the war may, if Dawson is right, have shaped millions of boys' understanding of their own masculinity. Perhaps girls' exclusion from these games, coupled with the nurse dolls and hospital games marketed at them, had an influence on girls' developing sense of their gendered identity. Boys became the men they were going to be, in part because of the military toys they played with as children. For them, playing at soldiers perhaps sparked an identification with forms of masculinity that encompassed the resolution of conflict through aggression. They learnt to be men by playing at being the type of men who fought. Similarly, girls grew up playing with toys that encouraged them to develop a sense of themselves as caring, nurturing women, future mothers, needed at a time when seemingly all the men in the world were fighting. The war encouraged the manufacture of toys sharply divided along gendered lines. There were no female toy soldiers, and no male Red Cross nurses. Children may have played with the toys meant for their siblings of the opposite sex, but this was not what was intended by the toy makers, or probably even the parents who bought them.

Toy soldiers

Kenneth Brown has linked the huge increase in production of model soldiers in Europe from the late nineteenth century to the rise of militarism in Europe before the First World War.[14] During the early years of the nineteenth century the market in toy soldiers expanded significantly as the availability of new materials and production techniques lowered manufacturing costs. This coincided with an increase in awareness and popular public support for Europe's standing armies, making the toys a popular choice for those who could afford them. At this time model soldiers were two-dimensional, flat metal cut-outs, but by the second half of the century German manufacturers were producing solid metal three-dimensional soldiers. By 1889 the value of toy imports to Britain had reached £714,828, most of this trade coming from Germany.[15]

In the 1890s, however, the massive expansion of toy soldier production in Britain began. A technological breakthrough by the British manufacturer, William Britain, adapted the casting techniques used to make wax doll heads to make hollow metal figures. These figures could be sold at half the price of their European rivals, and by 1900 Britains was producing over 100 different models. By 1910 it is estimated that roughly 200,000 figures a week were being produced by Britains alone.[16] The next few years saw the emergence of a number of other small companies, copying Britains' technique.

The craze for model soldiers also took hold amongst some adults. William Britain's son, Alfred, remembers that from as early as 1896 his father's firm was receiving regular orders for every new set from several 'gentlemen' buyers who appreciated their 'perfect modelling and correct colouring'. Amongst the adult collectors was H.G. Wells, who was so keen on the hobby that he even wrote a book on war-games to be played with the figures.

Little Wars was published in 1913 and set out a system of rules and suggested strategies for playing toy soldiers. 'Little Wars', Wells wrote, 'is the game of kings – for players in an inferior social position. It can be played by boys of every age from twelve to one hundred and fifty – and even later if the limbs remain sufficiently supple, – by girls of the better sort, and by a few rare and gifted women'.[17]

The book was popular and sales do not seem to have been hit by the advent of the 'Big' war the following year. Indeed, the British Library's own copy is inscribed with the dedication 'To John from Auntie May, Xmas 1914'.

But Wells was at pains to make clear that he suggests 'Little Wars' as an alternative, rather than a preparation for the real thing. At the end of the book he issued an entreaty to the posturing nations of Europe to avoid war, saying:

> How much better is this amiable miniature than the Real Thing! Here is a homeopathic remedy for the imaginative strategist. Here is the premeditation, the thrill, the strain of accumulating victory or disaster – and no smashed nor sanguinary bodies, no shattered fine buildings nor devastated country sides, no petty cruelties, none of that awful universal boredom and embitterment, that tiresome delay or embarrassment of every gracious, bold, sweet, and charming thing, that we who are old enough to remember a real modern war know to be the reality of belligerence.[18]

The problem, Wells believed, is that:

> I have never yet met in little battle any military gentleman, any captain, major, colonel, general, or eminent commander, who did not presently get into difficulties and confusions among even the elementary rules of the Battle. You have only to play at Little Wars three or four times to realise just what a blundering thing Great War must be. Great War is at present, I am convinced, not only the most expensive game in the universe, but it is a game out of all proportion. Not only are the masses of men and material and suffering and inconvenience too monstrously big for reason, but – the available heads we have for it, are too small.[19]

Despite this certainty, however, the book contains a puzzling contradiction. It contains an appendix for an adaptation of the rules of *Little Wars* to be used for Kriegspiel, war strategy games played by army officers in training. This was apparently in response to a demand for such an adaptation by military leaders who had written to Wells after the publication of much of his book in a magazine. But Wells saw no contradiction in deploring war and then offering help for the training of soldiers. He simply wrote:

> If Great War is to be played at all, the better it is played the more humanely it will be done. I see no inconsistency in deploring the practice while perfecting the method.[20]

That many parents should encourage their sons to play war games and master military strategy is not surprising, Brown believes, as toys have always been used as instruments of instruction and socialisation as well as amusement. Nicola Johnson, addressing imperial and nationalist influences on children's toys and ephemera during the nineteenth and early twentieth centuries, agrees. Parents gave boys toy soldiers not to encourage a martial spirit or foster aggressively patriotic play, but, rather, to prepare them for adulthood, as their sisters were being prepared through the gift of dolls and dolls' houses.[21] Boys from relatively wealthy families were often destined for a career in the military, so, just as their sisters had models of the future household they would be expected to run, the boys had a miniature version of their future to play with on the nursery floor.

This was perhaps particularly likely for children from military families. Henry Harris was given a selection box of Britains' soldiers by his father, a professional soldier, on his return from France in 1916. From that point on Henry's interest was keen, and when they later moved to Army quarters at Aldershot his weekly good-conduct reward was a box of Britains. Harris' scrupulous father 'was careful to keep a balance between the various arms and services, although I realise now that there was a bias towards his own cavalry regiment'.[22]

By 1918 Henry had perhaps 400–500 figures, which he would regularly parade on the floor to be inspected by the family's soldier servant. On a trip to Dublin towards the end of the war Harris met another boy and in their subsequent war games lost many of his most precious models. Harris' interest was no doubt strengthened by his own father's status as a real soldier. Indeed, the choice of the original gift of the soldiers by his father suggests a deliberate attempt to form a shared bond between father and son around the figures.

But family connections and a parental desire to see sons go into the military cannot alone explain the popularity of the soldiers. Indeed, sales figures suggest they must have been bought by many parents never intending a military career for their sons. Richard Church, whose father was a postman, remembers the excitement of playing with the toys as a child. He owned a fort, with various regiments of soldiers and a field gun which fired rubber shells a quarter of an inch in length. As a child of 11 in 1904 Church played alone with his figures, near to his mother, who was becoming seriously ill. He remembers that the game occupied him but that:

Behind this slaughter, however, and the momentary excitement it engendered, my mind was at work on its own more unique concerns, chief among them being my sense of foreboding as I watched my mother, furtively, from time to time.[23]

Playing alone and despite the worries over his mother's health, Church was excited by his toy soldiers. He could fight a battle, playing the part of both army commanders, using his fort and solitary gun, and become absorbed in play. He has noted how his soldiers had become more drab in appearance, dressed in the khaki of the recent Boer War, and that his one company of Coldstream Guards stood out in their bright uniforms. Church does not mention a particular interest in the military or the Boer War, yet he still owned and played with toy soldiers. This suggests that they were a common gift for boys, given perhaps because of their topical nature, but not necessarily indicative of particular parental approval or childhood interest in war.

Not all parents were so keen on the soldiers as toys, however, and, as well as nonconformists who had a tradition of hostility towards all things military (albeit a weakening one by this time), other parents were also raising concerns about their suitability. In 1888 the women's branch of the International Arbitration and Peace Society heard a speech by Oscar Wilde's wife that called for toy soldiers to be kept away from children for this very reason.[24]

This lack of civilian figures was not lost on all model enthusiasts. H.G. Wells bemoaned the lack of alternatives, despite his very public love for war games.

> Consequent upon this dearth, our little world suffers from an exaggerated curse of militarism, and even the grocer wears epaulettes. This might please Lord Roberts and Mr Leo Maxse, but it certainly does not please us. I wish, indeed, that we could buy boxes of tradesmen: a blue butcher, a white baker with a loaf of standard bread, a draper or so; boxes of servants, boxes of street traffic, smart sets, and so forth ... We have, of course, boy scouts. With such boxes of civilians we could have much more fun than with the running, marching, swashbuckling soldiery that pervades us. They drive us to reviews; and it is only emperors, kings and very silly small boys who can take an undying interest in uniforms and reviews.[25]

But the fact was that, in the years leading up to the First World War, toy manufacturers were in no mood to produce civilian figures. The build up of tension in the Balkans before the outbreak of war saw Turkish,

Greek, Montenegrin, Serbian, and Bulgarian armies produced for children's gratification. War sold, and toy manufacturers were well aware of this, a trade editorial remarking:

> Nine out of every ten boys until they are twelve years of age at least want to be soldiers, and the desire is much greater if there is a war in progress in some part of the world. The Balkan War caused an increase in demand for play soldiers and the market was fairly swamped with orders for these.[26]

Most products were designed as sets of opposing armies, and children were being encouraged to play games that pitted one side against the other, where someone won and someone lost. They were invited to play battles and wars where enemies fought each other to the bitter end, and where fighting was the whole point of the game. Whereas before they had had to rely on nineteenth-century wars to inspire them, with the outbreak of war in Europe their armies could become miniature versions of the real ones, perhaps representing absent fathers and brothers seeing action abroad. For the toys to be convincing and for the industry to thrive it was important that children continue to make this imaginative link between their models and the real thing. To foster this, Britains produced *The Great War Game for Young and Old* (1908), which contained photographs of their toys alongside ones of their real-life counterparts. Similarly, A.J. Holladay's 1910 book *War Games for Boy Scouts Played with Model Soldiers* urged children to 'try and realise what Lord Roberts and Lord Kitchener felt when in command of all those men in South Africa'.[27]

In the 20 or so years immediately before the First World War, then, Britain saw its market for toy soldiers expand dramatically, reaching production figures of between 10 and 11 million toy soldiers annually by 1914. Much of this growth was created by the new and innovative production techniques that saw British models supersede their German rivals in both quality and value for money. As the soldiers were marketed in box sets of varying sizes and quality, and the figures were also retailed individually, the toys could be enjoyed and afforded by a broader range of parents and children than ever before. This widespread popular interest was shared by adults as well as children, and spawned books on how to play strategic games with the models as well as others on correct uniform and the histories of the various regiments. They were given as gifts by parents and bought by the children themselves, sometimes because of a strong identification with military tradition, but also simply because they were fun and would be enjoyed.

And what was the result? Had the young men who volunteered for war in 1914 been unconsciously prepared for conflict by a childhood spent in pitched battles arranged across the nursery floor during this golden age of the toy soldier? It is hard to believe that such toys, coupled with the imperial adventure literature and youth group movements all aimed at children, could fail to have had some effect on young minds and their understanding of conflict and duty. And what of the children playing with the figures during the war itself? For them, at least, the games cannot have lasted long. By the end of the war and throughout the 1920s and 1930s parents turned against the figures as their sense of shock and loss turned gradually to revulsion at the idea of all things military. No longer would adults give their children model soldiers and encourage them to stage battles. Instead, companies like Britains turned to producing civilian figures, some of the most popular being farm characters and animals along with buildings and vehicles. But this was to come later – for first there was a war to be won and an enemy defeated.

War games

In fact, Britains only made eight new issues of model soldiers during the war, and at one time feared they would be forced to close as materials grew scarce. At the outbreak of war, however, toy soldiers were joined by a swathe of new products with a distinctly anti-German theme. While the August 1914 issue of the trade paper *Games and Toys* was still running advertisements for the *Journal of the German Toy Trade*, priced at 6s. 0d. per year, by September the mood had changed and the new issue was dubbed the 'British Empire Number'. British toy manufacturers, dominated for so long by their superior German rivals, were quick to cash in on the opportunity not only to have a dig at their competitors but also to steal their trade. As early as September 1914 a *Games and Toys* editorial was warning of a rise in the manufacturers' price of toys of between 10 per cent and 50 per cent, but was also extolling the opportunities for British business to replace banned German imports with British products.

The same issue carried adverts for Faudels Patriotic Favours, which included badges, buttons, flags and rosettes in the colours of the

Union Jack. Manufacturers were also swift to advertise their products as 'British Made by British Labour with British Materials – indeed, British Throughout'. Anticipating the glut of Christmas trade, the October issue carried an even greater number of hastily produced toys of the moment. For 1/- you could buy 'The Dash to Berlin' – 'the new and breathless game for winter evenings':

> All the excitement with none of the danger – that just describes this very latest British Table game which absolutely grips its players' interest from start to finish. You have the gallant Allies sometimes advancing, sometimes retreating holding their own, losing and winning, but gradually pressing onwards as in the great game of war itself.[28]

Other board games included 'Recruiting for Kitchener's Army', which retailed at 6d and consisted of a beautifully illustrated map of the British Isles over which players had to travel, collecting recruits along the way. The player to reach Dover with the greatest number of recruits was declared the winner. There was also 'Europe in Arms – an entirely new race game between the allied countries to reach Berlin', and the incredible sounding 'Berlin', an indoor golf game that came complete with putter and seven citadels.[29]

Other heavily marketed items were toy guns and pistols, and an October article urged manufacturers to fill the gap created by the absence of the German imports to produce top-quality substitutes:

> The war spirit is in the air, and wherever one turns will be found the troop of youngsters with paper hats and oddments of uniform, with biscuit box drums and wooden swords, parading the principal streets and drawing many a smile even from those who know too well the serious side of soldiering. These gutter urchins, for the majority of the street regiments are not much else, have a parallel amongst the children of the better classes, and these carry arms of a sort wherever they go, and quite a number are rigged out with air guns and pistols that fire a cap or discharge water.[30]

The 'war spirit' was certainly in the air for the writer Evelyn Waugh, who was born in 1903 and lived in Hampstead as a child. Here he describes a game he played with some local children:

"WAR TACTICS"

OR

Can Great Britain be Invaded ?

The only game acknowledged by LORD KITCHENER, Admiral SIR JOHN JELLICOE, Vice-Admiral SIR DAVID BEATTY and SIR ARTHUR GREY HAZLERIGG, Bart.

No other recommendation should be needed to induce dealers to stock this most skilful and interesting game.

"War Tactics"

is the Golden Game for a Silver Coin.

RETAIL PRICE,

2/6

Complete with 72 men, book of rules and playing board 19 in. × 24 in. when opened out. Printed in four colours.

It is a proved selling line throughout the Empire.

Not only is it a game for to-day, but a game for the future.

PLEASE PLACE YOUR ORDERS AT ONCE.   LIBERAL DISCOUNTS

Prompt deliveries guaranteed.   Send for sample and particulars to—

SOLE MAKER & PROPRIETOR: **ARTHUR RENALS, 2, Town Hall Lane, LEICESTER.**

Tel.—2287 Central.   ESTABLISHED 1858.   Tel. Add.—" Renals, Town Hall Lane, Leicester."

Please mention "**Games and Toys**" when writing to advertisers.

Figure 3.1   Advertisement for 'War Tactics' – board game produced by Lowe & Carr. *Games and Toys* December 1915

The Rolands became my constant companions. We lived in expectation of a German invasion. I do not know what put this idea into our heads. The alarm was not shared by our parents. In 1909 P. G. Wodehouse published *The Swoop*, which describes such an invasion foiled by a boy-scout. None of us certainly ever saw that work. The theme must have been much in the air of the youth of that time.[31]

The children called their group The Pistol Troop, made a camp in Hampstead Garden Suburb, and stocked up with provisions. Waugh remembers that they drew up a code of laws and ordained savage corporal punishments, never to be inflicted for their breach:

> We had some scuffles with roaming bands who attempted to enter our fort, whom we repelled with fists, clay-balls and sticks, but we were not provocative. We were reserving our strength for the Prussian Guard.[32]

In Tansley, Derbyshire, 13-year-old J. Leonard Smith attended the Herbert Strutt School. Smith remembers a particular game inspired by the war and popular amongst the boys:

> In the school playground there stood a mountainous heap of rubble which – if my memory serves me aright – had been left behind by builders after demolishing an old building prior to erecting a new wing when war conditions allowed. We called this 'Hill Sixty', this being the name given in war dispatches to a strategically placed hill on 'the Front'. This hill had been fought over, taken and re-taken time and again by the German and Allied Forces, with enormous loss of life on both sides. So, being boys, we too must have our Hill Sixty, and many were the tussles to dislodge the enemy – members of an opposing house – from their supremacy on top of that heap of rubble.[33]

Smith's remark about 'being boys' suggests that he might agree with those who consider war play to be boys' natural choice of game. He remembers that he and his friends felt they too 'must have our Hill Sixty', indicating that incorporating real adult battles into their games was not uncommon amongst his schoolfellows. They were excited by what they knew surrounding this bitter conflict for a coveted bit of ground, and felt that they too could fight as desperately for their own pile of rubble.

An added dimension to the game came with the participation of a group of Belgian refugee children who had joined the school. Smith writes that there was an aura about these children that is difficult to explain to anyone not of those times:

> Why they should almost have struck terror into the hearts of their opponents I still do not fully understand, but without doubt it was more than a psychological advantage to have them in one's own ranks when attacking Hill Sixty! Belgium at that time had been over-run by the Germans after a fierce resistance, and from their King downward the Belgian people were rightly regarded as heroes, and those refugee lads may well have felt that they had to maintain their country's reputation.[34]

Whether these boys had toy guns, or improvised with sticks they found lying around, the author does not mention. But their understanding of events in the real war inspired the game, with the children mimicking what they believed to be the behaviour of real soldiers. This was significant and profitable for toy manufacturers, and in an article entitled 'Toys and What They Teach' the educational value of toy guns was being stressed for this very reason:

> Toy rifles, air guns and similar model weapons are proving good selling lines throughout the country, and in conjunction with uniforms and helmets enable boys to make up in a very soldier like style...These guns, and other warlike toys all have the power to teach, and the drill of adults will for sure find itself duplicated by the youngsters...The hint conveyed by these youngsters should not be lost on retailers, for the smallest of boys will want some part, if not the whole, of a military outfit, which, of course, would not be satisfactory without a weapon.[35]

Models included the slight Warspite Pea Repeater as well as the more substantial Scout, Drake, Celt or Revenge, which used explosive caps for extra effect. There were double-barrelled guns like the Zulu or the Ajax, as well as repeating pea pistols capable of firing 20 shots in rapid succession. There was even the Little Dandy, a pea pistol and popgun in one. The guns were so realistic that, under the Defence of the Realm Act, a permit was needed to sell them or risk a five-pound fine.[36]

If children did not have toy guns to fire at each other they could buy any number of miniature guns to shoot at various representations of the enemy. These included a game with replica cannon to fire at model

... The absolute ...

ALL=BRITISH FIRM

Compocastles Ltd.,

108, Upper Street, London, N.   'Phone: 3338 North.

COMPOCASTLES' NEW GUN
(Patent Pending.)

Enormous Range.   Terrific Report.
Fires Rubber Shells.   Quite Harmless.

A magnificent model.   Stocks in preparation.

Particulars on request.

DREADNOUGHT

28 inches long - - **90/-** per dozen.

TOY FORTS, from 6d. to 50 Guineas.

CASTLES, DOLLS' HOUSES, MODEL COTTAGES.

NEW LINES.

Toy Rifles, Howitzers, Cannon, Engines, Pigeon Shooting Game, Mysteriscopes, Toy Bedsteads, Tunnels, Shelter Trenches, Camp Stools.

NEW LIST ON REQUEST.

Please mention "Games and Toys" when writing to advertisers.

Figure 3.2   Advertisement for Compocastles Ltd. *Games and Toys* April 1915

forts, trenches and German infantry, in which points were deducted if you hit the Red Cross tent.[37]

Britains toy soldier company produced perhaps one of the most horrible toys of the war, so gruesome in fact that it was discontinued

68

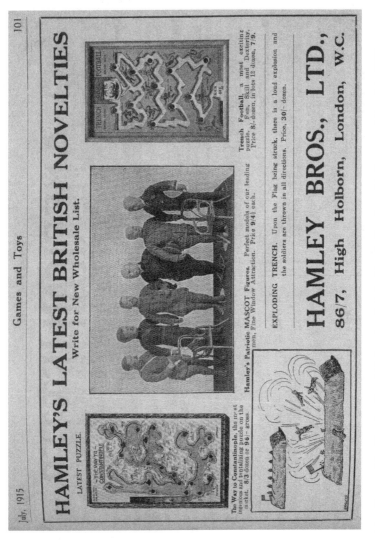

Figure 3.3 Advertisement for Hamley Bros Ltd showing Britains' 'exploding trench'. *Games and Toys* July 1915

almost immediately after its initial production, when it must have been realised that the British public did not quite have the stomach for it. The 'Exploding Trench' was roughly a foot long and made of cardboard and wood. It had a target flag which, when shot with one of Britains' 4.7 Naval guns, triggered a spring mechanism which hurled the toy soldiers inside into the air with an enormous bang. G.M. Haley, a collector who owns one of these very rare items, summed up the problem with the toy in a letter to the collectors' magazine the *Old Toy Soldier Newsletter*:

> Thousands of young men from the British Isles and the Empire were going to their deaths at this time... What self-respecting parents would allow their younger children to play with an 'exploding trench', no matter how innocently, when at the very same time as those nursery games, elder brothers were perhaps literally getting blown to pieces in the hell that was the war in France?[38]

Cheaper toys included card tricks and paper novelties in which the Kaiser would be made to disappear or look ridiculous. The Armstrong Boxing Appliance Company made boxing dummies with a new range to represent the Kaiser, Kitchener and others, while Dean and Sons made dolls including a soldier, a sailor, a midshipman, John Bull, a gunner and a boy scout.

The doll trade was another manufacturing group to take advantage of the absence of German imports to increase their productivity. Previously shipped from Germany, china doll heads were quickly added to the repertoire of British factories. So important was this change that the children's magazine *Little Folks* even ran an article on it called 'Christine – and all British' subtitled 'How they make dolls in England now' in their September 1917 edition. The story, which centred on the purchase of a new doll for the young Peggy, complete with exacting description of the process of manufacture, ends with the ecstatic Peggy leaving the shop carrying Christine exclaiming, 'I shall never want a *German* doll again'.[39]

Molly Keen's younger sister Ivy rejected a favourite toy when it was pointed out by her older brother that the lovely china doll she cradled was 'made in Germany'. Ivy, Keen writes,

> promptly divested it of all its clothes and hung it upside down in the gooseberry bush! We all tried to persuade her to take it down but she was adamant in this and refused to do so.[40]

There were also toy books with cut-out soldiers, and Messrs Gale and Polden Ltd published a series of toy books including *The British Army*

Painting Book, Our Foot Soldiers, Our Guns and Men and *Regimental Pets of the British Army*. The truly patriotic parent might also buy a Deans 'Patriotic Pinafore' so their child could dress in a replica military uniform.

The First World War had a positive impact on British toy manufacturing. At first forced, but then eager, British companies exploited the enforced absence of their German competitors from the British market to develop and sell their own versions of products that had long been dominated by the enemy. By promoting the purchase of their stock as a patriotic act, manufacturers and retailers exploited the pro-British sentiments of their customers to boost trade despite the rise in prices of between 10 per cent and 50 per cent in the immediate weeks after hostilities were declared. Companies quickly developed new lines in board and floor games based around the themes of war, and by Christmas 1914 families could choose from a range of products that allowed them to recruit their way across Britain or fight their way across France.

Trade editorials encouraged manufacturers to look around them at the children pretending to be soldiers outside in the streets. These children, from the more affluent homes at least, needed equipping with uniforms and guns, and companies that ignored this demand were sure to lose out. And if they did not want to be soldiers themselves then children could take the part of an army commander and fire miniature guns at fortifications and soldiers, where their bloodless victims could fall like heroes doing their duty for their imagined country. To keep up morale and feed the market for cheaper paper novelties, products were developed promoting a negative image of the Germans that children were invited to mock and despise. At the same time, dolls and uniforms allowed children to play as key British heroes and heroines of the war, forging an identification with the soldiers, sailors and nurses that may have stayed with the children for the rest of their lives.

Children were presented with a particular version of the war through their toys. Adults manufactured and purchased toys and games that featured the war as their primary inspiration to provide children with entertainment as well as lessons about the war. In turn, children were able to purchase their own cheaper toys and games, indicating that at least some of the demand for the toys was, indeed, shaped by the children themselves. We also know that some children played games re-enacting the war that didn't necessarily require any manufactured toys. They could improvise with objects they found lying around, or, indeed, play without any props at all. In these cases the war provided a narrative background around which the children created their own games without the help of any adult intervention.

Children's books

Late nineteenth and early twentieth-century boys' juvenile literature reflected the public school ethos of manliness, courage and patriotism. That tradition was consequently disseminated to grammar school boys and the working classes through the cheaper boys' magazines of the day, which followed similar themes. Tales of imperial adventure promoted a sense of British superiority and fostered a desire for adventure that some historians believe helped pave the way for the enthusiastic response to war in Britain in 1914.[41]

Boys' magazines were relatively cheap and enjoyed a wide circulation amongst the newly literate population. Those who had no access to the more expensive volumes of fiction received the message of masculine adventure and fair play through the numerous boys' magazines like *The Boys' Own Paper* and *The Captain*.

Lord Northcliffe's magazines had always addressed the concerns of its proprietor, and in the years before the First World War its pages were filled with stories that highlighted the need for a stronger army to repel invaders. Frequent stories about German attempts to invade Britain appeared between 1906 and 1914 in the *Boys' Friend, Boys' Herald, Marvel, Magnet* and *Gem*. The attempts were always unsuccessful, scuppered on various occasions by Boy Scouts, school boys and regular fictional heroes like Sexton Blake. This preponderance of stories that cast Germany as Britain's most likely adversary has led some to conclude that:

> If by 1914 the boys of Britain and the Empire were not raring to go and have a crack at the Kaiser it was certainly not the fault of Lord Northcliffe or his authors.[42]

While Kelly Boyd has noted that by the end of 1916 the publishers of boys' story papers had lost their enthusiasm for the war as a backdrop because of the lack of opportunity it provided for exciting narrative, the theme remained popular in book form.[43] Boys' fiction produced during the war continued and expanded upon the themes of imperial adventure to help inculcate in children an understanding and approval of the war based on the justification of Britain's participation and the superiority of her forces. Transposing the setting from an imperial colony to the Western Front, the stories were packed with adventure and intrigue for the hero from the start. Frederick Sadlier Brereton, a prolific writer of boys' wartime stories, and cousin of G.A. Henty, perhaps Britain's most famous nineteenth-century boys' fiction writer, continued to publish himself as Captain despite his promotion to the rank of Lieutenant Colonel. Mary Cadogan and Patricia Craig in *Women and Children First* maintain that younger readers generally believed the books to be authentic records of the writer's war experiences. In reality, they were often based on Boer War experiences and bore little resemblance to the actuality of the fighting in France.[44] Presumably Brereton kept his rank as Captain when publishing to give his stories added authenticity. If his readers were to believe that the stories were based on his own experiences of the war, then being promoted out of the fighting line and into the general staff would have left him little opportunity for seeing any of the fighting for himself.

War stories, like their imperial predecessors, were formulaic. Our young hero was always amongst the first to volunteer, has numerous close scrapes along the way and often manages to transfer regularly between different branches of the army, navy and air force, allowing him a full range of opportunities for heroism. British soldiers are always gallant, brave, strong and resilient, their German counterparts sneaky, underhand and cowardly. As in real life, many of the lead characters are young boys who have lied about their age in order to enlist, desperate to get out to France before the war is over and they miss their chance.

British participation in the war is supported in all stories, and young readers are often told the moral reasons for the fighting by characters in the books. The tone of many of their explanations is didactic, suggesting the authors recognised the importance of their message to young readers and were keen to leave them in no doubt about the legitimacy of the fighting. In Brereton's *With French at the Front* (1915), for example, the position is laid out in a conversation between two soldiers:

> She [Britain] could have stood aside, have hugged her tight little island and her numerous colonies and dependencies within her fleet, and sat down securely to watch this titanic conflict which Germany has commenced...But it [the treaty] bore Great Britain's signature. It carried the honour of millions of us, millions of simple, plain-dealing Britishers, with scrupulous minds and an idea of fairness and of what is proper far transcending ideas in the minds of Prussians. We had nothing to gain. We had all to lose – lives, ships, treasure – above all, that position in the world of protector of the weak which our sea power and our known peace-loving policy has gained for us.[45]

The fighting described in the books predictably bore little or no resemblance to the real thing. Authors and the public alike had little opportunity for learning about trench conditions other than from the newspapers or from returning soldiers. Newspapers wanted to sustain morale at home, and so did not dwell on the uncomfortable surroundings of the troops abroad. Returning troops were often reluctant to discuss their experiences with their family and friends, in part to spare them the horrors they were experiencing, but also, perhaps, to protect themselves from having to discuss at length things they would rather forget for their short time on leave. Equally, the reality of the grim stalemate on the Western Front provided little inspiration for exciting adventure fiction. For the books to sell, and for their message to be successful, it was no good having your hero sitting in a hole in the ground, up to his knees in mud, for weeks at a time.

Set on the battlefields of Vimy, Messines and Ypres, where some of the most horrifying battles of the war actually took place, Brereton's *Under Haig in Flanders* (1918) illustrates the artistic licence authors employed when writing. At one stage 'our hero' has, as usual, volunteered to undertake a dangerous raid into enemy territory:

> A spree indeed! It was a desperate and most adventurous undertaking. Not that Roger or Bill or the Sergeant thought of it in that way. They ate their supper with gusto, sat chatting for a while and turned in to sleep like children. Then, an hour before dawn, a sentry wakened them, and, having drunk a steaming cup of cocoa apiece, for comforts are not by any means non-existent in the trenches, the three made ready for a journey across no-man's land into the country of the enemy.[46]

We know from soldiers' testimony that in fact men often found waiting to take part in dangerous action one of the most difficult things to do. The anticipation and the fear prevented men from sleeping, or being able to eat, and instead forced them to confront the dangers they were facing. In the five months of 1916 that the British fought on the Somme roughly 500,000 British troops were killed, and little ground was won. According to Brereton, however, the battle went well, with the men fighting bravely and skilfully. Perhaps feeling unable to claim total success, he explains:

> It was not the capture of ground we sought, nor the destruction of dug-outs and defences; it was to drive a blow home to the heart of the enemy, to destroy the soldiers of the Kaiser, to break the strength of the German invader. That we went far to achieve that object there is no doubt.[47]

The 'comforts' of Brereton's war at the front included:

> Frizzling bacon, not to be beaten anywhere, bread that might have graced the table of a Ritz hotel, and jam that would be the envy of any housewife.[48]

As well as inspiring readers with an exciting and positive image of life in the army, children's authors were also keen to present the enemy as one worth fighting. If morale was to be sustained at home, government propagandists and pro-war journalists and writers knew that a sustained negative perception of all things German needed to be maintained amongst the British public.

Children's authors were always ready to exploit the negative attributes of their German characters, and German troops were depicted as both un-sportsmanlike and cowardly. The Germans were derided as fighting men, and their tactics were regarded as underhand. In Brereton's *Under Haig in Flanders* (1918) sniping, a tactic employed by both armies, is discussed by a sergeant in the trenches, who claims:

> It's a craze with them Fritzes. They like killing people in a dirty sort o'way, they do.[49]

Another common tactic was to portray German characters with cruel and nasty characteristics, in contrast to the British, who were always good and decent. When speaking of Germans held by the British, we are to understand from a character in Percy F. Westerman's *The Fritz Strafers* (1919), who has been captured by the Germans but is remembering German prisoners he saw on an English boat, that:

> In the matter of food and drink they fared equally as well as did their captors; if wounded they were given the best medical attention available, and their comfort was considered in almost every possible way. The ungrateful Hun, however, does not thank his captors for their little attentions. With the arrogance of his race he attributes his easy lot as a prisoner of war to the fear of the British as to what might happen to them when Germany is victorious. And on their part the British have got to learn fully – as they are beginning to do – that the only thing the German fears is the force of armed might.[50]

In addition to the negative attributes of the Germans as soldiers, the Britain of wartime fiction was overrun with German spies, many of them appearing as ordinary citizens who had been living there for years. The popularity of this theme can perhaps be understood by the fact that it gave authors the opportunity of suggesting to children a way in which they could help win the war. The fact that your next door neighbour could be a German spy meant that children could take part in some amateur sleuthing of their own. The spies, it appears, were not hard to spot, and they are usually suspected because of some small but obviously un-British trait like a grumpy nature or a cruel smile. In a story written by Angela Brazil, in which a German girl, who later turns out to be perfectly innocent, is relentlessly pursued by two over-zealous classmates, we are told that she was first suspected because:

> Her pink and white colouring, blue eyes and twin braids of flaxen hair were distinctly Teutonic; the cut of her dress, the shape of her shoes, the tiny satchel slung by a strap round her shoulder and under one arm – so unmistakably German in type – the enamelled locket bearing the Prussian eagle on a blue ground, all showed a slightly appreciable difference from her companions, and stamped her emphatically with the seal of the 'Vaterland'.[51]

Brazil was amongst a small number of authors writing about the war for girls, and it is interesting to note the differing representations of roles for women in boys' and girls' fiction. The girls who appear occasionally in boys' fiction are delicate and sensitive, and rarely get to take part in any of the action. Even when female characters are allowed to display enterprising characteristics, as, for instance, Gladys in Brereton's *With French at the Front* (1915), it is not for long. Gladys Fairleigh is a young English woman, working as a governess in Germany when the war breaks out. She is being helped to leave the country by the book's two male heroes when they are all arrested. Overhearing that the two men are to be shot the following morning, Gladys determines to rescue them by crawling through a ventilation shaft. Yet, after this unusual burst of heroics, we are told that Gladys reverts to type:

> Indeed Gladys had been wonderfully plucky up to the moment when everything depended on her alone. Now that she was with the two gallant men who had protected her from Berlin, when, as it seemed, there was no longer need for personal exertion or for nerves to be braced, she sat down suddenly on the floor and buried her face in her hands. They saw her shudder and heard a stifled sob.[52]

Female authors, on the other hand, writing for girls, were quick to take advantage of the changing social climate in which women were taking up the opportunities of more and varied work outside the home and for the war effort. The heroines, albeit fewer in number than their male counterparts, work on the land, in the factories and as army and ambulance drivers. Brenda Girvin's eponymous heroine in *Munition Mary* (1918) single-handedly foils a German spy-ring attempting to sabotage the newly employed female labour force in the munitions factory owned by the fierce Sir William. Sir William is so prejudiced against women working outside the home that he will apparently walk up several flights of stairs rather than get into a lift operated by a woman. Mary's colleagues initially blame the sabotage on Sir William himself, but the loyal Mary fights to prove his innocence and ultimately captures the Germans. Throughout, however, Girvin is at pains to let her readers know that Mary lost none of her 'womanliness' despite taking up men's work. It takes all of this to win round Sir William, who eventually concedes:

> This girl had shown intelligence and capability yet...yet surely nobody could be more feminine than she was. Her tears on that awful night – only a very feminine woman would have given way to tears as she had. Her chutney making! His grandmother had made chutney. She had all the charms of his grandmother. He had been wrong to think that when a girl did a man's work she lost her womanliness.[53]

Other characters are more impatient with the slowness of social change, and in *A Transport Girl in France* (1919), by Bessie Marchant, the heroine Gwen delivers a scathing attack on British attitudes. Gwen is working on a farm, having volunteered early in the war. She has applied for a transfer, however, as she knows her superior driving skills could be used 'to free another man for the front'. When her request for a transfer is refused, she laments to a friend:

> My dear Daisy, the war may have changed us in a few things, but in downright bedrock essentials we are just where we were – just as stodgy and stick-in-the-mud as ever. No wonder the Germans used to beat us in trade. No wonder we find them so hard to beat at warfare.[54]

Gwen eventually gets her transfer, and by the end of the tale is in France driving for a general. But Gwen's character continues to push the boundaries of traditional fiction, and our inevitable happy ending sees her literally lifting the man she loves out of a collapsing building.

Girls' fiction was not remarkably ground-breaking, although it does hint at the possibility of a greater role for women in the post-war world. Girls were being exposed to a broader range of experiences open to women through their fiction, as they were through their involvement in the Girl Guides.[55] Women writers always presented energetic, capable and competent heroines in their books, and, while the girls may have been keen to retain their 'womanly charms', they did at least roll their sleeves up and get stuck in when given the chance. Interestingly, none of the stories focuses on a nurse heroine, one of the most high-profile ways in which women were contributing to the war, and one of the most popular forms of toy doll marketed at girls. Perhaps this was because the authors felt that nursing was too domestic a role for their heroines. Life in a hospital, with its endless rounds of bed making and wound dressing, while undoubtedly noble, hardly provided the opportunity for heroines to foil spy rings or catch Germans. Perhaps this rejection of the role of nurse was also an unconscious attempt by the authors to counter the overtly domestic and feminine toys produced for girls by men. There were no toy female ambulance drivers or munitions workers or land girls; instead, girls were only offered the nurturing, caring, motherly role of nurse. Women writers wanted a proactive role for their heroines, where they took part in the war as active participants, rather than responding to its horrors by caring for others wounded in action.

Picture books for younger children illustrated the various branches of the armed forces as well as the flags of the various allies. Several books taught the alphabet while explaining some of the basic elements of the war. *The Child's ABC of the War* (1914) begins:

> A stands for Austria, where first was hurled
> The bomb that was destined to startle the world.
> B is for Belgium, brave little state
> So valiant for Honour so reckless of fate.
> C's for our colonies, loyal and true
> Bringing help to their mother from over the blue ... [56]

Our Soldiers – An ABC for Little Britons (1916) was a large picture book, each letter accompanied by a vivid colour illustration depicting the scene described. It ended:

W for the WOUNDED, tenderly borne Out of the fighting line bleeding and torn.

X for the RED CROSS; noble their task – To help the poor wounded is all that they ask.

Y for the YEOMEN, Stalwart and brown, Sons of the Colonies, True to the Crown.

Z for the ZEPPELIN, floating on high, laden with bombs to drop from the sky. Are you afraid of it? No, not I![57]

The same company also published the similar *The Royal Navy – An ABC for Little Britons* (1915), which had the following poem on its back cover:

> Now I am seven I mean to go
> On the Iron Duke with Jellicoe;
>
> I'll do my best to fire the guns,
> And sink the warships of the Huns.
> When I'm grown up, perhaps I shall
> Sail as a gold-laced admiral;
> I'll wear a sword and cocked hat fine,
> And never go to bed till nine.[58]

There were other books of poetry aimed at children, including the beautifully illustrated *What the Elephant Thinks of the Hun* (1918) and Nina MacDonald's *War-Time Nursery Rhymes*. Dedicated to D.O.R.A., the book contains a foreword which states that, although British children had been spared the face-to-face confrontation with war experienced by many Belgian and French children, they had nonetheless been exposed to the war because of their fathers' and brothers' experience. There can, therefore,

> be no possible objection to dealing, from the nursery rhyme point of view, with certain conditions brought about by the war. It is good that certain facts of the war should be impressed upon the mind of childhood, and there is no better means of impressing them than by the nursery rhyme. The facts dealt with in nursery rhyme remain with us from our childhood to our old age.[59]

What the facts that should be 'impressed upon the mind of childhood' are, the author does not say. But when we consider the content of some of the poems it becomes clear that the hope is the children will learn to hate the German enemy and fight for their destruction.

The book contains a total of 58 popular nursery rhymes adapted to the theme of war, dealing with every aspect of war, from food shortages to military training. Perhaps one of the most gruesome is the horrible 'The House that Jack Built':

> This is the house that Jack built.
> This is the bomb
> That fell on the house that Jack built.
> This is the Hun
> That dropped the bomb,
> That fell on the house that Jack built.
> This is the gun,
> That killed the Hun,
> That dropped the bomb,
>
> That fell on the house that Jack built.
> This is the man in Navy-blue,
> That fired the gun,
> That killed the Hun,
> That dropped the bomb,
> That fell on the house that Jack built ... [60]

Storybooks for younger children included the charming *At War!* written and illustrated by Charlotte Schaller. The story, published in 1917, is about Bobby, a little French boy whose father has gone off to war. Bobby and his friends set up their toys and fight the war in their playroom and garden, while Bobby's younger sisters Zezette and Jacqueline start up a hospital to care for the wounded. As none of the boys want to play the part of the 'bosch', the children stick nails in the top of toy skittles to represent the spiked helmets of the enemy, then shoot them down with toy cannon.

The children also help with the war effort, and, after Zezette and Jacqueline have knitted gloves and hats for the brave soldiers in the trenches, Bobby slips into the parcels packets of tobacco, cigars, cigarettes, pipes and matches, which he buys with the pennies out of his money-box. The children are also shown writing to their father, which they do every day with great care.

Bobby tells of his fine army, always in fine trim; Zezette and Jacqueline of the wounded that they are caring for in the hospital. They put their best into their letters, for they know what pleasure it gave Papa who was fighting so bravely to protect them.[61]

The inside covers of the book are covered with slogans like 'Long live England', 'Long live the Triple-Entente', 'Long live our Cavalry' and 'Long live India'.

This book has a particular place in the heart of one man, who was born just before the start of the war and who had a father fighting in France. James Thirsk, who grew up in Beverley, near Hull, during the war, remembers this book particularly in his autobiography:

I knew this book before I was able to read the text and Jean [elder sister] would have told me the story... How we came to have this book I do not know; Dad may have bought it in a bookshop in London on his way home from France, on leave. It was for us a treasure worth more than gold and it remains for Jean and me one of the happiest memories of our childhood. It was, after all, the story of three children who, like us, had a father fighting at the Front.[62]

Thirsk, who says that he has not seen the book since he was a young child, remembers every detail of it, down to the colour of the illustrations. It has become a significant part of his memory of the war years, perhaps because he and his sister identified so strongly with characters in the book. As a very young child, Thirsk perhaps understood little of what the war was really about. All he knew was that his father was gone and that those around him were worried for his safety. Having a book about other children whose father had also gone to the war perhaps helped the Thirsk children to cope with their father's absence. They would see that they were not alone and that other children were facing similar fears to theirs. The fact that he could not read himself, and that his elder sister read the tale to him often, suggests a private bond existed between the siblings around the book. Both now remember it fondly, suggesting that they remember their reading together happily, perhaps because they were sharing the same experience, one that separated them from their mother but brought them closer together.

Conclusion

Increasing prosperity, the introduction of compulsory schooling and restrictions placed on the employment of children meant that more and more families in the late Victorian and Edwardian periods found that they had children at home and money to spend on them. Improved production techniques and a reduction in transport costs meant that new and better toys were appearing on the market all the time in the years leading up to the outbreak of war. War-themed toys and fiction were a major part of this industry, as during the nineteenth century there had been an increase in the production and consumption of toy soldiers and an explosion in juvenile fiction heavily associated with imperial adventure. In this way Brown, Walvin and others have argued that an acceptance of, and even desire for, war was created in the period immediately before the First World War.[63] When war came, however, children were exposed to even more vehemently aggressive attitudes through their toys and games than had been the case previously. The emphasis of these products also shifted subtly, moving away from their more overtly imperialist themes and onto strongly anti-German attitudes, in line with the fierce position of the popular press.

In the cheaper card and paper games and juvenile magazines, as well as the more expensive products and books, children were presented with the very definite position of Britain in relation to the war. There was to be no confusion; Germany was at fault and had to be stopped by the British. Children's fiction glorified the war while presenting it as the natural outcome of a confrontation between the unscrupulous Germans and the moral, fair-dealing British. The formulaic stories described the conflict in simplistic language of right and wrong; positive British characteristics were juxtaposed against negative German ones in order for all children to understand whom to support and who the enemy was. A lack of public understanding about the reality of trench fighting meant that the wildly inaccurate descriptions of army life in the tales went unchallenged by parents, who lacked the knowledge to contradict the images of exciting battles, daring raids and sumptuous food.

Girls' fiction pointed towards, rather than demonstrated, the possibility of new opportunities available to women after the war. Authors rejected the more domesticated role of nursing for their heroines, choosing instead to place them in the action as drivers, industrial workers and spy catchers. Despite this, most characters still held on hard to their 'womanliness'; they dutifully supported their brothers in uniform and strove to find love and secure themselves a future as wives and mothers. For younger children there were nursery rhymes, alphabet books, colouring books and picture books which all embraced the themes of war, sometimes hiding little of its brutality from their young readers. The pleasanter ones encouraged support for the war by depicting British soldiers alongside colonial troops and allied forces to show children how

Britain was being joined by friends in her quest to defeat the enemy. Children's books and toys were designed to keep up morale at home by poking fun at the enemy while strengthening support for the British forces. Children were encouraged to hero-worship anyone in uniform and not question the reason for war or the fate of those who fought in it.

But this relationship was not all one way. The children were not simply passive recipients of these messages. There were many influences outside the toys and books specifically aimed at them that also helped contribute to their understanding of the war and informed their play. As we have seen, children did not necessarily need any particular product to play war games; fights and battles inspired by the war could be played by imaginary armies with imaginary guns. If there had been no war toys, it is likely that children surrounded by the real war would still have been inspired to act it out amongst themselves. For children wanting a connection to their absent fathers and brothers, re-creating the war through play, or reading tales of battles in fiction, was perhaps the closest they could come. As we saw with James Thirsk, he revelled in a tale he could not yet read because it was about other children, like himself, with a daddy fighting the war.

4
Children in Uniform

Introduction

Perhaps the most visible way in which British children were mobilised
for the war effort during 1914–1918 was through their involvement in
organised uniformed youth groups. Boys and girls, usually between the
ages of about 12 and 18, were routinely employed by hospitals, local
authorities and central government, while others contributed by collecting, making and preparing everything from clothing to splints and
bandages for the British troops. Their efforts were directed by the organisers of Britain's youth groups, who saw the war as a great opportunity
to bring home to their members the need for the self-discipline, obedience and self-sacrifice that were behind so much of their teaching.
The children were to be of service to their country in its 'hour of need';
they had been trained for it and, more importantly, the desire to do it
had been instilled in them. And they did want to do it. Members of the
Boys' Brigade, Boy Scouts and Girl Guides all threw themselves enthusiastically into the war effort – they relished the opportunity to become
involved, to feel they were 'doing their bit'. What is interesting is that
the children did not always interpret their role in quite the same way as
their leadership intended, in a manner that suggests the children wanted
even more responsibility than they were being given. For female youth
groups the war had a transforming effect; they proved their worth, leading to greater public acceptance and an acknowledgement that girls and
women, if allowed the right training, could contribute to the defence of
the nation.

To understand how and why Britain's youth groups were so keen to
mobilise their members for the war, we must understand the climate
in which they were created. Britain was under threat from increased

industrial and military competition, particularly from Germany, and the Boer War had raised serious questions about the country's capacity to defend its empire. In the late nineteenth century social investigators like Charles Booth and Seebohm Rowntree had identified levels of poverty that prompted fears of permanent racial degeneration.[1] Many imperialists felt that the country was going soft through neglect. Britain was becoming complacent. So, just as it was important for the nation to take steps to remedy its physical failings, it was also important to address the moral direction in which it was headed. If Britain was to remain a strong imperial power, then the rising generation must be prepared to take up their role as imperial leaders.

It is within this context of anxiety about the nation's health, wealth and imperial well being that we see the emergence of a number of uniformed youth groups during the late Victorian and early Edwardian periods. Initially these groups were targeted at working-class boys. Boys, it was felt, lacked discipline. They lacked moral fortitude and their attempts to behave as 'men' were often misguided, leading them towards loutish behaviour and crime. They needed to be taught to respect society, to recognise the need to sacrifice their own self-interests for the common interests of the British Empire. They needed to be taught 'manliness' as defined within the public school ethos of self-discipline, obedience and fair play.[2] Girls, on the other hand, needed to be trained as mothers. The rapidly declining birth rate, and the challenges posed by the expanding women's movement, prompted imperialists to fear that women were endangering the empire by refusing to carry out their essential role as mothers to a new generation.[3] So, as girls attempted to join groups like the Scouts, attracted by the exciting freedoms suggested in their literature, they were diverted into sister organisations that instead reined in their enthusiasm, and set them on a path to becoming good mothers and companions to men.

Influenced by social Darwinism, many youth group leaders saw the condition of human existence as a ceaseless battle for survival and considered young people to be the ammunition of the future. For them, the First World War represented the epitome of that struggle for survival. By considering how they directed young people's involvement in the war effort, therefore, we can begin to understand what values and attitudes they felt it important for children to learn in order to equip them to carry on that struggle in the future. Here discussion of male and female youth groups has been separated, partly because their leaders kept them so separate. The intention was to teach boys to be men and girls to be women, each with their own particular role. However, it will be noted that many of the concerns of their leaders were the same. It was feared that both boys and girls were in danger of moral degeneracy, and both were taught, before the war and during it, the importance of self-sacrifice, discipline and obedience, amongst other things. The fundamental point for both was that they should be trained to be useful citizens, keen to give service to their country and their empire.

The problem with boys

The identification of youth, and particularly male urban youth, as a significant social problem to be tackled by experts on 'Boy Nature' emerges at the end of the nineteenth century, at the same time as the recognition of the existence of adolescence as a separate stage of life.[4] Until the late nineteenth century, any discontinuity between childhood and adulthood was largely reserved for the upper and middle classes, whose children enjoyed an extended period of youth at preparatory and public schools, and finally at university. This period of what some historians have termed 'self-conscious boyhood' was celebrated in boys' magazines like the *Boys' Own Paper* as well as being frequently eulogised by those (men) lucky enough to have experienced it.[5] For working-class youths, on the other hand, the end of childhood came with the transition from school to work. This occurred at around 13 or 14 for the sons of skilled workers, who often spent some years at a secondary school, but ended at 11 or 12 for the sons of the unskilled, who received no formal education after elementary school.

The expansion, and inherent problems, associated with 'boy labour' in all the major cities began to trouble middle-class philanthropists, who saw the plight of large numbers of boys employed in dead-end jobs, with no training or prospects for future employment, as a contributing factor to the perceived rise in juvenile delinquency. In fact, Charles Booth's pioneering turn of the century study of life and work in London identified 'boy labour' as a special characteristic of the city's economy.[6] These boys, outside the controlling influence of school, responsible employer or, increasingly, religious influence, were deemed to represent a serious threat to the moral and social future of the nation. They were falling through the gaps of decent society. For a few years after they left school they had work. After contributing to the household economy they might still have money in their pockets and were experiencing the greater degree of freedom that bought them. When they were fired from their jobs (to be replaced by another school leaver who could be employed at a lower rate of pay) they were liable to spend an extended period of time without employment. During this time, with no structure to their day, and no direction in their activities, it was felt they could be tempted into bad behaviour and crime. And what good were these boys to the empire? None, if they were allowed to hang around on street corners, smoking and becoming involved in petty theft. What they needed was direction and structure in their lives.

If the future of the empire lay in the hands of these youths, it became increasingly clear to imperialists that more care must be taken to ensure that young people realised and accepted this responsibility. Lord Meath and the National Service League (NSL) launched campaigns to promote national service and the Empire Day movement, while the empire was portrayed in juvenile literature as a source of inspiration and adventure to young people in Britain. Young men and women of the middle classes were encouraged to become military leaders, missionaries and teachers in the colonies, while working-class youths were encouraged to emigrate as domestic servants and soldiers. But, this was not enough. If the nation's youth represented the empire's future they could also represent its demise, and imperialists were not prepared to leave that future to chance.[7]

The Boys' Brigade

The Boys' Brigade was founded in Glasgow in 1883 by Sunday School teacher and local businessman William Smith, and was the period's first uniformed youth movement aimed at attracting the sort of boys it was believed most needed reforming.[8] Smith had been a member of the 1st Lanarkshire Rifle Volunteers for almost 20 years when he decided to try using his training in the Volunteers to set up a Brigade programme for his class, as a method of controlling the behaviour of the boys. It was a success, with 59 boys signing up immediately. Smith quickly saw the advantage of a scheme of Christian training for boys that bridged the gap between the age of about 13, when boys tended to drift away from Sunday school as they began work, and 17, when they were old enough to join the YMCA. It was during this period, it was felt, that many working-class boys began to run wild, becoming 'hooligans or street loafers'.

The stated object of the Boys' Brigade, then and now, is 'The advancement of Christ's Kingdom among Boys, and the promotion of habits of reverence, discipline, self-respect, and all that tends towards Christian manliness'. It was a non-denominational movement based around

Christian teaching and military drill, which quickly spawned Anglican, Catholic and even Jewish branches across the country. By 1900 there were 906 companies nationally, catering for over 41,000 boys.[9] Springhall, Fraser and Hoare note the growing connection between religion and the military in late Victorian Britain in their study of the Boys' Brigade. They believe that the growth of what they term 'Christian militarism' had been evident in Britain since the Crimea and the Indian Mutiny of the mid-Victorian era, and point to the religious literature that used stories of evangelical generals to create the image of Christian soldiers as heroes. In addition, they cite the years of peace and relative stability as contributing factors to the softening of the military image to one of colour and pageantry. This, combined with the adventure stories written for children and featuring both real and imagined military heroes, created an atmosphere in which military drill, titles and leadership added an air of respectability to what Smith was trying to do in the minds of many Glaswegian parents.[10]

This greater acceptance by the public of military values could also be seen as a response to perceived threats to male dominance. John Tosh has suggested that, during this late Victorian era, the partial militarisation of what he terms 'hegemonic masculinity' in Britain served to reinforce the indispensability of manly attributes at a time when women's demands for greater political, educational and social involvement appeared to 'pose a challenge to traditional patriarchal assumptions'.[11] The increased visibility of women and women's issues was explicitly linked in the minds of imperialists with the falling birth rate. Some women were seen to be deliberately turning their backs on their role as mothers, and demanding new roles within male society. For those wanting to stem the tide of female emancipation, the strong identification of the soldier as an ideal form of masculinity was one way to emphasise social difference along gender lines. Indeed, one argument often employed by anti-suffragists in the early Edwardian period was that women, who could take no part in the defence of their country, should have no right to determine policy that instructed men to fight. Men earned their right to vote through the basic fact that they could be called upon to sacrifice themselves for their country if need be.

Like the leaders of other uniformed youth movements, Smith was able to see that by giving youths activities and a structure that appealed to them he would be able to deliver his aims in a way that was more likely to be well received. The desire that boys be taught to be 'manly' was not necessarily at odds at all with what the boys themselves wanted to be; it's just that Victorian social reformers had very specific ideas about what the right kind of 'manliness' entailed. Smith understood this:

> All a boy's aspirations are towards *manliness*, however mistaken his ideas may sometimes be as to what that manliness means. Our boys are full of brave earnest desire to be brave true *men*; and if we want to make them brave, true *Christian* men, we must direct this desire into the right channels...We must show them the *manliness* of Christianity.[12]

Using military training to instil Christian values did not sit comfortably with everyone, however, and the Boys' Brigade attracted some fierce criticism from some nonconformist churchmen. One such man was the Revd John Brown Paton, retired principal of the Nottingham Congregational Institute, who brought the idea of a non-militarist Boys' Life Brigade before the National Sunday School Union in 1899, persuading them to adopt it as a national organisation with himself as the first president. The Boys' Life Brigade operated for 27 years, after which it merged with the Boys' Brigade. Throughout it sought to give the boys the same training in obedience and discipline that the Boys' Brigade achieved through military training, using life-saving drill, gym and first aid training. By 1914 there were over 15,000 boys and 400 companies in the Life Brigade, mostly connected with the English Free Churches.[13]

The Boy Scouts

In general, Sir Robert Baden-Powell, hero of the siege of Mafeking during the South African War, it would appear that Edwardian society had the perfect candidate for the leader of another military youth group. However, when Baden-Powell formed the Boy Scouts in 1908, he, at least publicly, had very different intentions for the direction of his new movement. Baden-Powell was born in 1857 into a well-connected, professional, middle-class family. He had an intensely devoted relationship with his mother, who encouraged competitiveness amongst her children and was ambitious for their careers. Biographers have suggested that the foremost influences on Baden-Powell's attitudes in later life were his experiences at his public school, Charterhouse, and as an officer in the British Army. At school he was not an academic achiever, but joined numerous societies and clubs and developed a love of the outdoor life. In the army Baden-Powell was suspicious of formal, orthodox military training, believing that it did little to help train really good soldiers.[14]

Baden-Powell was an imperial patriot and believed, as did many others, that the physical deterioration of the British race, as highlighted by the 1904 Report of the Physical Deterioration Committee and exacerbated by the falling birth rate, and the waning interest in the fortunes of the empire, were signs of national decadence, and posed a real threat to the future interests of the nation. According to Springhall, Baden-Powell was further spurred into action by his fears that the Liberal government's welfare policies were weakening the public's motivation for self-help, claiming:

> Free feeding and old age pensions, strike pay, cheap beer and indiscriminate charity do not make for the hardening of the nation or the building up of a self-reliant, energetic manhood.[15]

Impatient with partisan politics, Baden-Powell was attracted to the then fashionable concept of national efficiency.

National efficiency won the attention of people of widely differing political allegiances, and was seen as a way to reverse the trend of moral and social degeneracy that was threatening the security of the empire. The concept appealed to those with social Darwinian beliefs, who felt that a strong British race was necessary for the maintenance of empire, as well as to Fabian social imperialists like Beatrice and Sidney Webb, who sought to secure their social reforms by persuading Liberal imperialists that the interests of a great empire were best secured by raising a strong imperial race.[16]

In drawing up his system for Scout training, Baden-Powell was heavily influenced by the American youth leader Ernest Thompson Seton, whose movement of Woodcraft Indians began in 1902. Seton's scheme centred around building up boys' character through learning techniques of woodcraft and the observation of nature, and fitted in well with Baden-Powell's own emphasis on the importance of tracking skills in army training. Baden-Powell's dislike for more formal methods of military training was to have a strong influence on his vision for the Boy Scout organisation. In drawing up his system of training, he eschewed the idea that military drill, or in fact drill of any kind, could produce the kind of boy the empire needed. Instead, Baden-Powell believed it was character training that was required for boys who had not had the benefit of a public school education, and therefore knew nothing of the spirit of citizenship that would produce a future generation ready to take on the responsibilities of imperial leadership.

The hidden curriculum of the public schools aimed to produce boys loyal above all else to their school and the ideals it espoused. It produced men willing and eager to serve and even die for their country, and to preserve the status quo when it came to the structure and workings of Victorian and Edwardian society. This, then, is what Baden-Powell wanted for working-class boys too. John Springhall and Michael Rosenthal see in this attempt at social control the sinister face of Scouting and other organised youth movements, where what amounts to the indoctrination of children was dressed up as entertainment. 'Wrapping his deeply conservative social ideals in an appealing and exciting movement', Rosenthal explains,

> he [Baden-Powell] achieved the formidable goal of creating an institution that could be embraced not only by those whom the social system was designed to support, but also by those largely excluded from its advantages.[17]

Organised Boy Scout activities appealed to some urban working-class boys, who had little opportunity for the excitement of camping trips and outdoor adventure in their normal lives. They were encouraged to embrace a movement that recognised individual achievement as well as promoting team spirit, and accept the importance of 'character training' by proving themselves responsible, useful young men. By training these working-class youths to be obedient, hard-working and self-sacrificing, Baden-Powell was seeking social cohesion, whereby everybody understood and accepted his place in the social order, and worked hard in the interests of the nation.

Others have disagreed with this social control theory of youth movements, pointing to their popularity and ability to attract young people from diverse regional, religious and class backgrounds as evidence that their aims could not have been so narrow.[18] Although I am more convinced by Springhall and Rosenthal's arguments, what the debate really highlights is the way historians have tended to concentrate on the youth groups' prescriptive strategies, rather than the practical realities of the organisations' efforts or the experiences of the young people themselves.[19]

Source material relating to children's experiences or the individual and local practices of youth organisations is scarce. Reconstructing a history purely based on participants' experience, therefore, would be difficult, because of the large number and variety of schemes operated for Britain's youth and the devolved nature of leadership at local level. Existing histories have identified youth culture in part through their focus on the aims and intentions of youth group founders, and the advice given out from headquarters. This has often produced a history that assumes that adult concerns automatically translated into children's experiences, and can imply an agenda that does not always reflect what the children themselves perceived their involvement to be about. This chapter, by contrast, explores both adult direction of Britain's youth movements in the years before and during the First World War, and also, as far as possible, what that wartime experience meant to the children themselves. It uses the accounts of individual youth group branches to understand the ways in which children interpreted the instructions they were given, sometimes following them and sometimes rejecting them, in their attempts to support the war effort.

Little soldiers?

The question of militarism, which is central to the discussion of the involvement of British youth movements in the war effort, has dogged these movements since their creation and continues to preoccupy historians today. Were groups like the Boy Scouts and the Boys' Brigade paramilitary organisations masquerading as peace-loving troops teaching nothing but moral fortitude and Christian manliness? Or were they in fact covert attempts, led by imperialists and National Service League supporters, to produce young men ready to serve as soldiers in the Regular Army or Reserves? The evidence is conflicting, but when you look at the histories of individual local groups, at what the children actually did, it becomes clear that, whatever the official position of the leadership, the experience of individual troops could be quite different. During the First World War, particularly, we see children involved in a huge range of activities designed to back up the war effort, some of them closely allied to the military. This allows us to understand how difficult it was in practice for local grass roots groups to distinguish between what activities were helping win the war in a non-military capacity, and what would be considered too militaristic for their leadership.

The fact that the Scouts, Boys' Brigade and Church Lads' Brigade were led by soldiers, wore uniform, learnt discipline and obedience, and in some cases drilled with weapons, yet have always defined themselves as staunchly non-militaristic, is what has always confused attitudes in this debate about the role of militarism in youth groups. The problem is made more difficult because of the loose interpretation of the word militarism. How do we define it as a concept? Do youth groups have to actively seek to encourage their members to want to serve in the armed forces to be considered militaristic? Or is it enough to positively model soldiering through the teaching of drill and outdoor survival skills? Can a child wear a uniform, carry a weapon and hold a military rank without being encouraged to absorb military values? The leaders of the major Victorian and Edwardian uniformed youth movements certainly claimed they could, but many commentators, at the time and since, have disagreed. By looking at the writings of youth group leaders and comparing them with the experience of children at grass roots level, this chapter will attempt to untangle this debate.

Although the Boys' Brigade carried all the trappings of a military group, uniform, military ranks and drill with rifles, their emphasis on the religious motivation for their existence was always their main defence against charges of militarism. It was claimed by the Brigade that the drill and ranks were merely a way to interest the boys and to teach them self-discipline. To militarists, however, the Boys' Brigade's methods fitted in well with their ideas to encourage service to empire and military training. From 1900 onwards there were an increasing number of organisations and individuals campaigning to strengthen the imperial ideal in Britain. Amongst them was Lord Meath, later the Boy Scout Commissioner for Ireland, who founded the Empire Day Movement and the Boys' Empire League, which sought to propagate the imperial message through schools. Others, like Lord Milner and Lord Roberts of the NSL, toured the country warning of Britain's fate if the nation failed to prepare itself for the military threat posed from abroad, and advocated conscription as the only answer.

These fears for the security of the empire were partially recognised by the Liberal government, and in 1907 the Territorial Forces Bill of the Secretary of State for War, R.B. Haldane, was passed. The Bill reorganised Britain's volunteer forces and brought all Officers Training Corps and Cadet Corps work under the control of the War Office. A portion of the Bill that proposed compulsory military training for boys at elementary school was rejected, following strong opposition from Ramsay MacDonald and the Labour and radical Liberal MPs. Haldane did, however, seek to bring all uniformed youth movements under War Office control, to act as feeder organisations for the new Territorial force.[20] This possibility of coming under War Office control was put to the youth groups as an attractive choice, as failure to become a part of the scheme carried the penalty of a withdrawal of all previous financial and military assistance from the War Office. The Boys' Brigade, however, consistently refused the offer between 1909 and 1911, although, as we shall see, they were later to relent.

The Boy Scouts, still only in their infancy at this time, also rejected the government's proposal. In all public statements and documents Baden-Powell and the Scout organisation always maintained their non-militarist standpoint. Distinguishing between war scouts and peace scouts, Baden-Powell always stressed that his Scouts were peace scouts, partly because he was aware of the negative connotations any military-style organisation would have in the minds of the prospective parents of just those sorts of boys he hoped to attract to Scouting. From the beginning Scouting's biggest critics were trade union leaders, working-class parents and Labour Party leaders, who distrusted attempts to organise youths into uniformed movements or introduce military drill into schools. At the Seventeenth Annual Conference of the Independent Labour Party in Edinburgh in 1909, Keir Hardie moved a resolution calling for an end to the building tensions between Britain and Germany, the eventual abolition of war, and declared the Conference's 'unabated opposition to all attempts to foster military customs in our schools or to impose compulsory military service upon the people'.[21] Labour leaders attacked the Scouts regularly in the press, so Baden-Powell was well aware that he needed to do what he could to minimise the appearance of militarism so as not to further alienate working-class parents.

Despite this, from its earliest writings, the Scout movement saw preparedness for war and the Scouts' role in any war as central to the very point of its training. Along with training in the importance of following orders and maintaining discipline, Scouts were also told of their responsibilities in case of war or invasion by the enemy. From its inception as an organisation, Scouting stressed the importance of service, service to country and service to empire. The children were to be trained to be useful, and, within the context of pre-war fears over imperial rivalry and the threat from Germany, that meant they were to be useful in a time of conflict. Baden-Powell's claim, then, that he was training peace scouts seems hard to reconcile with the fact that he was preparing them for war. Michael Rosenthal, a biographer of Baden-Powell and historian of the Scout movement, also sees this problem:

> [T]he notion of the Scout as a serviceable citizen trained to follow orders in wartime is at the heart of Scouting. Whether this makes him a war Scout or a peace Scout, or whether a willingness to defend one's country is the best way to express detestation of war is beside

the point; what matters is simply that Scouting holds out before us a model of human excellence in which absolute loyalty, an unbudgeable devotion to duty, and the readiness to fight, and if necessary die for one's country, are the highest values.[22]

There was also confusion amongst local scout troops themselves over what counted as militaristic activity. From their earliest days in 1908, Scouts in Chiswick had organised their own rifle training, taking lessons from the father of one of the boys, and some members even went on to compete in national shooting competitions. However, one former Scout from the troop recalls that they felt there was nothing inherently militaristic about what they were doing; perfecting their shooting skills was simply a way to instil discipline and build character. What is interesting is that the writer recalls that the practice was discontinued after the end of the First World War. Presumably this was because shooting was too closely associated with the military war, and perhaps parents and even the boys themselves had lost their enthusiasm for it as a form of character training.[23]

Even more strikingly, Scouts in Derby before the First World War were awarded proficiency badges for infantry training, and some troops had been known to give demonstrations of rifle and bayonet drill. So skilled were these boys in military drill that, once the war itself broke out, some of the troops were to be found marching round the district leading trainee soldiers in their first experience of route marching.[24] What is clear from these examples is that troops at a local level interpreted their training instructions in different ways. While Baden-Powell might have advised troops not to take part in military drill or train with weapons, boys and their Scoutmasters at a local level did not always follow these directions. If the boys themselves were particularly interested and had access to some local training, as those in Chiswick had, they took advantage of it because they saw no conflict between that and the rest of their Scout training. Likewise, if a local Scout leader with military experience passed that on to his troop it was because he believed he was carrying out the aims of Scouting by preparing his boys to be useful citizens of the empire.

Despite continually denying any connection with militarism, the Boy Scout Association was repeatedly challenged by some of its own members over the issue, and on several occasions in the early years breakaway groups formed when the executive failed to take their concerns seriously. The first of these disputes arose in 1909, when the Scout Commissioner for London, the liberal aristocrat Sir Francis Vane, complained that NSL leaders had populated the Scout Council. Vane felt that executive control of the youth movement had been given to soldiers and conscriptionists, whose aims were in stark contrast to Ernest Thompson Seton's woodcraft philosophy. After a tense couple of months in the winter of 1909, when it looked possible that the entire London membership might withdraw from the movement, Vane was forced to resign, later taking charge of the more peacefully inclined, but short-lived, British Boy Scouts.[25] Interestingly, when the NSL eventually disbanded in 1921 it handed its assets of £12,000 to the Boy Scout Association, as being the body which most 'successfully teaches the ideals of citizenship of which Lord Roberts' scheme was a part'.[26]

A second split occurred when, in 1915, several leading members of Scouting in the Cambridge area broke away to establish an organisation to oppose the military stance the Scouts were taking in the war. The naturalist Ernest Westlake joined them as leader, and in 1916 they set up the first group of the Order of Woodcraft Chivalry. Westlake and his son Aubrey closely modelled their movement on Seton's Woodcraft Indians, but were also heavily influenced by the American social Darwinist G. Stanley Hall's theory of 'recapitulation'. This theory sought to apply Darwinian biological ideas to the educational psychology of adolescence, believing that every developing adolescent 'recapitulated' the cultural history of the human race in the stages of their own physical and mental development. To incorporate this into their movement, a system of training was developed to allow children to live through the earlier stages of mankind in order that they might appreciate and understand the present stage of evolution.[27]

Another London Scout leader, John Hargrave, Commissioner for Camping and Woodcraft at Scout Headquarters, started the Kibbo Kift Kindred in 1920. Hargrave was unhappy with the strong association the Scout movement had had with the war effort, and sought to form his own movement on more socialist, pacifist lines. The Kibbo Kift did not survive for long as a youth movement, however, as its leader became immersed in the Social Credit movement and then the Greenshirts, a militant section of the League of the Unemployed.[28] The 1925 Woodcraft Folk have been more successful, and still survive today. Begun by members of the Co-operative movement, this organisation has been the closest thing to a socialist Boy Scout/Girl Guide group, and was certainly popular in the decades after the war, when anything associated with militarism came to be distrusted by parents. However, it never had anything approaching the membership of the

Boy Scouts, who also sought to distance themselves from their more imperialist, militarist standpoint of the pre-war years by emphasising the importance of internationalism and class harmony.[29]

Clearly, the question of militarism confused attitudes amongst those interested in youth movements then just as it does now. Despite repeated assertions from the leaders of the Boy Scouts and the Boys' Brigade, and the continual refusal to accept War Office support, both groups suffered from breakaway movements concerned that militarism was creeping into the schemes. But we cannot be convinced that this perceived strain of militarism came solely from the military leaders of such groups; in fact, it appears that some of the most overtly military activities often originated at local level. Local boys led by individual Scoutmasters were taking it upon themselves to practise shooting, bayonet drill and marching, despite instructions from headquarters that they were not to do so. This suggests that, despite the strong and charismatic leadership of both Baden-Powell and Smith, the huge scale of the movements they spawned meant that uniformity of practice at local level could never be achieved. By the outbreak of war in 1914 there were just over 60,000 boys in the Boys' Brigade and over 153,000 Scouts.[30] Both groups were deliberately attempting to mould the character of their members to produce useful, patriotic boys, prepared to take on the responsibilities of citizenship. It is unsurprising, therefore, that in the immediate pre-war years, when so much press and political attention was being paid to preparedness for war, young boys should want to learn the skills to make themselves useful soldier–citizens.

The war

Whether militaristic or not, at the outbreak of war British youth groups threw themselves into the war effort. The Boys' Brigade immediately offered its help to the government, but felt the need to defend itself against accusations of joining in military activities in the October 1914 edition of the *Boys' Brigade Gazette*. Describing their offer of service as not only a duty but also a privilege, the *Gazette* goes on to say:

> Our offer was unconditional; to have excluded from our offer purely military duties would have been unnecessary, because the age limit of our Boys makes it impossible for them to be employed directly either as Territorials or in the Regular Army ... To have excluded everything that could be called in a sense 'military duties', would have made our offer valueless.[31]

The *Gazette* also stressed that the Brigade was determined to maintain its principles of non-militancy and to retain the full liberty to work independently of government, as in normal times. As we shall see, during the course of the war this independence was challenged and eventually, in part, relinquished by the Boys' Brigade.

At the start of the war the boys of the Boys' Brigade were urged by their leaders through the *Boys' Brigade Gazette* to help their mothers at home, do extra tasks without being asked and not complain about any shortages of food. As the war progressed, however, their services were increasingly needed outside the home as messengers and orderlies, in ambulance troops, and to signal the 'all clear' after air raid warnings.

The Boy Scout Association used its monthly magazines (*The Headquarters Gazette* for Scoutmasters and *The Scout* for boys) to pass on instructions as to the sort of work that Scouts might become involved with now that war had been declared. Scout duties, which they were already largely trained for, would be designed so as to release men for the more arduous tasks of war. Their scope, it was claimed, would be non-military, and would fall more in line with police work that could be directed by the Chief Constable of each county. Specifically, Baden-Powell, in the very first month of the war, suggested that the work of the Boy Scouts would include:

a) Guarding and patrolling bridges, culverts, telegraph lines, etc., against damage by spies.
b) Collecting information as to supplies, transport etc., available.
c) Handing out notices to inhabitants, and other duties connected with billeting, commandeering, warning etc.
d) Carrying out organised relief measures amongst inhabitants.
e) Carrying out communications by means of despatch riders, signallers, wireless.
f) Helping families of men employed in defence duties, or sick or wounded etc.
g) Establishing first-aid, dressing or nursing stations, refuges, dispensaries, soup kitchens etc., in their clubrooms.
h) Acting as guides, orderlies, etc.[32]

The speed with which local Scout organisers were able to put into practice Baden-Powell's suggestions can be gauged by this letter sent in to *The Scout*. The boy, a Scout from Hampstead, North London, was on holiday in Sandgate, Kent, when war broke out, but responded to the notices posted around town asking Boy Scouts to report to the local

Figure 4.1   A Boy Scout military dispatch cyclist at work
Source: Imperial War Museum.

headquarters of the Red Cross Society. Having taken his uniform with him on holiday, the boy was included in the activities of the local troops:

> First of all I delivered some official documents, and then went and bought some cloth and flannelette for pyjamas, shirts etc. I then

assisted in shifting about a hundred chairs from the Memorial Hall to the Bevan Convalescent Home. After this we rigged up beds in these two buildings and the Devonshire Nursing Home. So we have now got three hospitals.

A spy was collared by two boys of the 3rd Hythe (Shorncliffe) Troop yesterday, and another was caught in Sandgate today – a patrol leader and I gave the report to the Post Office.[33]

Baden-Powell also suggested that Scouts and Sea Scouts could assist the coastguards in watching the nation's estuaries and ports. Their organisation by counties under their Commissioners, and even their distribution in small units under Scoutmasters all over the country, was seen to be a great strength, making mobilisation easy, and putting the Scouts in a strong position with their existing knowledge of the local area and conditions. Even when Scouts had no knowledge of an area they could be put to good use. Some troops were away from home at their annual camp when war was declared, but many were asked to help immediately in the place they were staying. The 4th Streatham Sea Scout troop were at camp in Leatherhead over the August Bank Holiday, and one member has recalled:

Immediately high adventure came to the lads for they were each given a whistle by the local police sergeant and told to guard the railway line at the end of the field . . . However all was well and the Territorial Army arrived after 3 nights and the '4th' boys were commended by the officer for their courageous act in helping to defend their country.[34]

To Baden-Powell it was inconceivable that the government would not jump at the chance of using such a well-trained and reliable force. Because of the implications of their war work, Baden-Powell felt confident that:

they will be excused from school attendance by the Education Committees and from work by their employers.[35]

They were not, and throughout the war Boy Scouts undertook their work in the evenings and at weekends. The only exception to this was in York, where Scouts were in such demand by local officials and public bodies that the local Education Committee agreed to the setting up of a Scouts' Temporary Day School, where Scouts would be available for duties for one week at a time, attending school at all other times.

Baden-Powell wanted his Scouts to understand what he saw as the positive lessons that could be learnt from war. He believed that:

The Damoclesian sword of war ever hanging over a country has its value in keeping up the manliness of a people, in developing self-sacrificing heroism in its soldiers, in uniting classes, creeds, and parties, and in showing the pettiness of party politics in its true proportion.[36]

For Baden-Powell, then, a people could be incited to work together for the common weal, sacrificing their individual, or class, concerns, if sufficiently afraid for the future of the nation. More importantly, in terms of Scouting's ideology, it proved the worth of their motto to 'Be Prepared'. The present conflict proved to the pre-war doubters of Germany's threat that the country must guard itself 'not merely for what may be probable, but for what may even be possible'.[37] As well as being prepared to be of practical use, the war was the ideal opportunity for Scouts to practise self-sacrifice, just as the soldiers abroad were being asked to do. An editorial in the *Headquarters Gazette* ran:

I like to tell my boys that in some small way they can in spirit, if not actually in person, lay down and protect a wounded soldier. They can voluntarily suffer hardship like good soldiers by some simple acts of self-denial. They can give up their beds and sleep on the floor when beds are required for hospitals. They can at least dispense with sheets and sleep in blankets.... The certain result of happiness for the boys themselves is not an inducement to be held out to them, but will follow in due course.[38]

And so 'character training' was to be achieved by teaching the boys to find happiness through self-sacrifice and self-denial. The example of soldiers, prepared to give up their lives in the service of their country, was held up as the epitome of successful character training, and young boys were urged to live up to the sacrifice the older generation were making for them.

Already, by September 1914, Scout Commissioners and Scoutmasters had mobilised their boys, offering their services, free of charge, to various government departments and regional bodies. Baden-Powell congratulated them on this effort, claiming that their hard work meant that the Scouts had, in fact, mobilised more rapidly than the Defence Forces, assuming the preliminary guarding of the coasts, telegraphs and railways until the others were ready to take over the duties. For Baden-Powell this was a great achievement. Despite the fact that the Defence Forces presumably had far greater numbers to organise as well as a broader range of concerns, Baden-Powell took pleasure in comparing his own force favourably with the nation's adult force. He wrote:

> This is a great feather in our cap and has once more drawn the grateful appreciation of the authorities; it has given us another definite step in progress in the form of the official recognition of the Scouts as a National non-combatant force.[39]

Fears that the enemy were planning to sabotage the water supply appear to have been rife, with many histories of local Scout troops reporting that their members were posted to guard reservoirs and waterworks. For one patrol the monotony of the work was broken one evening in the first month of the war. In Glasgow, Scouts Alex Beckett and Arthur Blair were guarding the Milngavie waterworks when Alex spotted a man climbing over the perimeter wall:

> The man had not gone far when Scout Beckett stopped him and asked him to show his permit. This he was not able to do nor would he give information about himself. The Scout asked the man to write down his name and noticed the German script of the letter B. Scout Blair arrived on the scene and water-works staff were alerted.[40]

The local paper later reported that the man was a German schoolmaster on holiday in Scotland and that he had been transferred to the custody of the army at Maryhill Barracks. After that follows an unsubstantiated report that he was shot later trying to escape from military custody in Edinburgh.

In recognition of the prompt and significant initial contribution by Boy Scouts across the country, the Scout uniform was formally recognised by the Government as the uniform of a public service, non-military body on 10 August 1914. With the announcement of this in the Scout press came the very stern admonition from Scout Headquarters that no Scout or Scout officer in uniform must on any account carry arms. However, again local groups interpreted these instructions differently. The 1st Chiswick Scout troop had been at camp in Westgate near Margate when war was declared. As the camp was very close to St Mildred's Seaplane Station, the troop had immediately offered their services there and had been accepted. Unlike other groups whose work away from home ended when the summer camp broke up, boys from Chiswick, who were no longer at school, were asked to stay on at the Seaplane Station (for which they were paid a shilling a day). Part of the boys' work involved patrolling the camp in the evenings and at week-ends; what is unusual is that they did this initially wearing full infantry fighting equipment – rifle, bayonet and 150 rounds of ammunition. Because they found carrying everything too heavy, all non-essential equipment was later omitted, although the boys continued to patrol with ten rounds of ammunition. One of the Scouts involved, Jack Hewson, reported later that he knew of the attitude of the Boy Scout Association towards its members carrying arms, but that he consid-ered his role to be an exceptional case 'and under similar circumstances would do the same again'.[41]

What is unclear is whether these Scouts patrolled with arms at the request of the seaplane garrison or whether it was a decision they took themselves. The garrison was staffed with about 50 Royal Naval Air Ser-vice personnel and 25 men from the Royal West Kent Regiment, and it seems likely that it was from one of these forces that they received their arms. It is clear, however, that they knew that what they were doing went against the principles of their movement, but they were willing to carry arms anyway. Bearing arms, to these Scouts, in the same way as the soldiers doing the same job seemed like the right thing to do. They believed that they were performing a military duty for their country in a time of war, something they had been trained to do, and then asked to do by the military authorities where they were stationed.

The Secretary of State for War Lord Kitchener saw, like Baden-Powell, the benefit of the war for Scouting, feeling that it provided the ideal opportunity both for Scoutmasters to show boys the real meaning and value of all their training, and for giving boys the chance to see it for themselves. Kitchener's thoughts were relayed to the Scouts in the September 1914 edition of the *Gazette*. They were told of his belief that there was a need for the manhood of the nation to come forward at this critical time, and of what he believed could be the value of the assis-tance of boys who were wholehearted in their work and could be trusted to carry it out to the very best of their ability. The Scouts, Kitchener declared, 'were a great asset to the nation'.[42] Such high praise, from so magnificent a war hero as Lord Kitchener himself, must have been very eagerly received by the boys engaged in Scout work, and the ready use made of them by government departments, hospitals and the like encouraged them to behave as was expected of them and help the nation in its time of need. Frank Hinton, a Sea Scout from Portishead, remembers that he and his fellow Scouts were put to work collecting everything from scrap iron to old rubber, as well as gathering herbs for medicinal purposes. He recalls that the Scout Association rewarded war work with a War Service Badge and that

> we all worked hard to get one of these coveted little discs showing that the wearer had put in 80 or 100 hours war service.[43]

The sadness for Baden-Powell was that Scouting had not begun 20 years earlier, for, if it had, he believed that there would have been an even greater response than there was to the country's call for defenders. There would have been a body of men already trained in discipline, initiative, self-reliance, resourcefulness and, most importantly, self-sacrifice, ready to jump at the chance to fight.[44] In the light of this sentiment I find it hard to believe that the philosophy behind Scouting was not, at its heart, a military one. To claim that you are not training future soldiers, but still to be sure that you would produce them, seems an odd certainty. But perhaps Baden-Powell could separate in his mind the instilling of patriotic sentiment and the desire to serve your country from the likely outcome of such teaching – enlistment in the Territorials or Regular Army. Indeed, as we have seen, some Scouts did not even wait until they had left the movement before they became involved in serving in a military capacity. At local level at least, there is evidence that the boys considered themselves a military force and would gladly have carried arms on a permanent basis had they been allowed.

So keen was Baden-Powell to have the Scouts prove useful during the war that he even offered to send a battalion of cyclists for service abroad as messengers, but the offer was declined by the Commander of the British Forces in France, Sir John French, on the grounds that the bad weather was likely to make conditions impossible for bicycles. Baden-Powell was prophesying as early as October 1914 that his Scouts would probably be called upon in the future to play a more vital role. While at present the army only wanted larger men of 19 and over, Baden-Powell explained, writing to his Scouts, it was likely that the time would come when the standard would be lowered to include younger men of smaller size. Already, he said, in Germany young fellows of 16 were being pressed into the ranks, and Britain soon might follow, at least for Home Service. To that end he said:

> I want all Scouts to Be Prepared for this, and to have our 'Bantam Battalion' ready, so that the moment the door is opened we can step in with a corps already trained for service.[45]

Baden-Powell invited every Scout between the ages of 16 and 18 to send in his name to his Scoutmaster as willing to serve if called upon; those boys should then be grouped into patrols, trained in rifle shooting, judging distance, signalling, pioneering, entrenching and drilling in accordance with infantry training methods. This scheme became known in 1915 as the Scout Defence Corps, which, Baden-Powell claimed, represented neither a shift in the movement's methods nor the beginning of a process that would turn the whole movement into a cadet corps run along military lines. He had, he said, taken the advice of a number of gentlemen who were, like himself, averse to military training as education for boys, and they all agreed, saying that:

> in the present national emergency, when the country is staking its very existence against the imposition of militarism over Europe, there is no harm in helping the older boys to prepare themselves for the defence of their homes, if need be.[46]

Baden-Powell's aim in setting up the Scout Defence Corps was to protect Britain from the threat of a German invasion, something he continued to urge both the country and his Boy Scouts to 'Be Prepared' for. It was believed that, in the event of an invasion, the Scouts, if properly prepared at once, could be of great national value, by acting both to allay the panic of civilians and to aid the machinery of the relief effort. The boys, therefore,

> should be taught to be prepared for the worst; to think out every situation that is likely, or possible, to occur, and be impressed with the fact that their duty is to observe discipline and keep a smile on, even in the worst of circumstances, in order to reassure the more frightened.[47]

Scouts should be detailed to all the leading authorities and, in case of invasion, cyclist patrols should sleep at their headquarters so as to rally all Scouts in case of emergency. Before an invasion Scouts could distribute warnings to inhabitants and organise their evacuation from certain areas, along with their wagons and livestock. After an invasion they could be organised into search and rescue parties as well as fire brigades to aid in the relief work.

It is hard to read these suggestions for the preparation and training of children to take such a substantial role in the organisation of the nation in the event of an invasion without feeling that those who advocated such preparations were exposing those in their charge to unnecessary risks. Baden-Powell, and the many other retired soldiers who made up the administration of the Scout Association, appear to have longed for some action in which their troops could take part. They urged their Scouts on and on in their training, suggesting more and more central positions for them within the Home Front war effort, ultimately positions which risked their lives. What if the Seaplane station in Margate had been attacked by German warships, or the German schoolmaster the boys in Glasgow apprehended had been violent? The whole point in involving these boys in the work that they did was that both the Scouting authorities and the military authorities believed that the threat from the enemy was real. Baden-Powell wanted to train young boys to be of service to their country in the future, but what he actually provided was children to serve their country in the present. The fact that Britain wasn't invaded should not obscure the fact that the Boy Scouts were expected by their leader to play a critical role if it was – and no doubt they would have been keen to do so themselves, regardless of the danger.

Perhaps mindful of fears on the part of parents that their children were being proposed for such dangerous roles, Baden-Powell even went so far as to issue a statement on 'What Scouts Could Be Shot For', claiming that their duties:

> if essentially non-combatant and designed to help their fellow-countrymen rather than to fight the enemy, do not render Scouts liable to capture or summary punishment at the hands of the enemy. Their uniform would be a protection to them like that of police.[48]

By December 1914, 1,400 Scouts had been retained by the Admiralty for duty as coastguards, following their call up as Navy Reservists. It was estimated that some 100,000 more were officially employed in government departments and hospitals.[49] In addition, returns from February 1915 announced that already 3,300 Scouts had joined the Scout Defence Corps, prepared to defend their country if called upon to do so.[50] From 1916 there were renewed calls from the War Office for the country's uniformed youth movements to become affiliated with the County Territorial Association as part of the nation's Cadet organisation. The unanticipated length of the war meant that there was increasing support for this as the patriotic option amongst some in the youth groups' leadership. Others took a more pragmatic approach, believing that recognition was one way to secure existing membership and encourage recruitment amongst boys who might otherwise just join their local cadet corps.

The cadet scheme, with its rigid reliance on mechanical drill, did not give enough prominence to Baden-Powell's idea of character, and he claimed boys trained by it ended up as worse recruits into the army than those with no training at all:

> In my own mind the boys of the country have a very definite place in the war – in the war that comes after this war – namely, in the struggle for industrial and commercial success which is going to raise our country out of the havoc brought about by the existing crisis, and which will consolidate for us tomorrow the results of victories won by our men in the field today, and will compensate for our losses.[51]

That war would probably continue for the next 10 or 20 years and would be won, Baden-Powell felt sure, by the country whose citizens were equipped for the work ahead. To that end, he felt that the nation should be concentrating on training the rising generation in individual character, technical efficiency and physical health. With this foundation he felt they would make the most efficient citizens and equally, if need be, the most effective soldiers. But to dress young men up

> in khaki and to teach them to play at soldiers under the allurement of the existing war fever, is, to my mind, to trifle with a very serious situation and with a very big national opportunity.[52]

The Boys' Brigade, on the other hand, was tempted by the idea of recognition as cadet corps, and in March 1917 the executive polled all companies for their opinions. Of the companies that replied (29 per cent did not), it was noted that over 74 per cent were in favour of any company being permitted to apply for recognition, subject to a guarantee being given by the Territorial Force Association concerned that there would be no interference with the religious and social work of the Brigade, and that only those nominated by the Brigade would be accepted as officers. Of those who were not in favour, most were entirely against, but some advocated delay in taking any definite step until after the war.[53] Consequently, the executive decided that, whilst these numbers did not warrant a recommendation that the Brigade as a whole should become cadets, support was so widespread that permission should be given to individual companies to apply for recognition without damaging their position in the Brigade.

Springhall, Fraser and Hoare, in their history of the Boys' Brigade, argue that the Boys' Brigade was worried about losing potential recruits to the secular cadet corps. The total number of boys in the Boys' Brigade fell from about 60,000 in 1914 to 43,000 in 1919, which suggests that this decision had little impact in attracting boys to the movement. By allowing the individual companies to accept recognition, the Boys' Brigade created an association with the state's military muscle that was to prove unpopular in the post-war years as many parents' reaction to the war turned to revulsion.[54]

Martin Dedman has described the Scouts' role in wartime as 'peripheral' and likened their work to that of women, designed to free men for the fighting.[55] While that may have been the position of the Boy Scout and Boys' Brigade leadership, in reality the children's work became much more than that. Children were relied upon by government offices, hospitals and the Post Office, as well as local military authorities and the police, who all recognised the potential for utilising such a large number of usually unpaid volunteers. When you consider the thousands of children who were organised by their troop leaders to guard bridges, deliver messages, sound the 'all clear' and so on, and who read the words of their leaders exhorting them to 'Be Prepared' or 'Be Steady', it seems unlikely that they themselves would have seen their role as peripheral. Indeed, as we have seen, some children embraced the chance for an active military role, believing that it in no way went against the principles of their movement. In fact, the organisations themselves also went to great lengths to make sure that the children's work was recognised, whether it be through recognition as a non-combatant force or a cadet corps, or through the award of a War Service Badge.[56]

Throughout the war young boys were trusted with important work by government departments, hospitals and the police, and this was purely because they had been trained for such work. Groups like the Scouts, the Boys' Brigade, the Church Lads' Brigade and others instilled in their members the importance of discipline, obedience, patriotism and self-sacrifice, and so successful were they that their members could be employed in such work. They were too young to serve in an overtly military capacity, though no doubt some of them, as well as their leaders, would have been more than willing to do so, but they nonetheless played an important part in the organised work of the Home Front.

The Girl Guides

When a band of self-styled 'Girl Scouts' gatecrashed the 1909 Boy Scout Rally at Crystal Palace, Baden-Powell initially showed little interest in their enthusiasm. When it emerged, however, that several thousand girls had in fact registered themselves with Headquarters as 'Boy Scouts', it became clear that some provision would have to be made for them. For Baden-Powell it was not desirable for the movement to become a mixed one. He foresaw the disgust of his boy members at having their movement hijacked by their sisters, as well as the disapproval of polite society at having girls take part in such manly activities in the company of hordes of boys.

The answer, then, was a separate organisation, to be run alongside the Scouts by his sister Agnes, with the same ideals of character training for the new generation, but with differing methods. In 1909, therefore, Baden-Powell published a pamphlet entitled *Girl Guides: A Suggestion for Character Training for Girls* and in 1912, with his sister Agnes, another one entitled *The Handbook for Girl Guides or How Girls Can Help Build the Empire*. In these pamphlets the Baden-Powells outlined what they saw as the problems and solutions for the female youth of the country. As with male youth, the problems lay in a decline in moral standards, and an increase in juvenile crime. The problem of getting good servants and the need for girls to be trained to become useful without becoming hard and unwomanly were both issues it was felt could be addressed by the system of training proposed for the Girl Guides. Most of all, girls, as future mothers of the sons of the empire, needed strong moral and patriotic training in order for them to be a positive influence on men.

As with the Boy Scouts, it was not certain at first whether the training would become a movement in itself, and in the 1909 pamphlets it is suggested that Guide training could be taken up by other female youth organisations, or perhaps as a cadet branch or feeder to the Territorial Organisation of Voluntary Aid. The suggestion was that every girl, of whatever social class, should be given practical instruction in hospital nursing, cooking, home nursing and ambulance works as well as moral instruction in religion, chivalry, patriotism and courage. It was stressed that this was best achieved through means that really appealed to girls, but that care should be taken not to encourage a girl to become a 'rough tomboy'.

The threat of invasion and the need to populate the colonies with good British stock are prioritised in the specific aims of the Girl Guide training. The 1909 pamphlet states that Guides would be trained:

1. To make themselves of practical use in case of invasion by being able to find the wounded after a battle; to render first aid; to transport them to hospital; to improvise ambulances, hospitals etc; to make hospital clothes; to cook; to nurse, etc.

2. To prepare themselves for colonial life in case their destiny should lead them to such; including camp life, farming, gardening, house-keeping, cooking, and so on.
3. To make themselves generally more useful to others and to them-selves by learning useful occupations and handiwork, and yet retaining their womanliness.[57]

The system proposed to cater for girls between the ages 12 and 16, but their organisation was going to have to be significantly different from that of boys. Whereas boys were urged to get up their own troops and then find a suitable adult willing to serve as Scoutmaster, it was felt that this level of freedom and initiative was not appropriate for girls. Instead, they were to wait for a local ladies' committee to initiate the groups, thus making it clear that the girls' activities were to be super-vised and structured appropriately from the first. If girls were to become guides and comrades to the nation's men, it was imperative they retain their womanly refinements and reserve. Having bands of unsupervised girls climbing trees and camping out was hardly likely to persuade the nation's adults that Baden-Powell's scheme was designed to train women to be practical and womanly.

Another reason that the character training for girls needed more leadership from the top down, as it were, had to do with class. For Baden-Powell, there was what he termed 'a bit of a gulf between the delicate lady of the castle and the fighting slattern of the slums', and he clearly had no intention of bridging it.[58] While men, of what-ever class, were equalised and unified through sports and work and war, they never, according to Baden-Powell, 'attain the angelic height nor the degraded depth that women do'.[59] Thus, while the train-ing laid down for Boy Scouts could be almost universally applied, training for girls must be altered appropriately to suit their feminine nature, which varied according to status. According to the 1909 pam-phlet, the training had to be administered with a greater degree of discrimination, for:

> you do not want to make tomboys of refined girls, yet you want to attract and thus to raise the slum girl from the gutter. Its main object is to give them *all* the ability to be better mothers and guides to the next generation.[60]

Thus, in the years before the war, the initial enthusiasm of girls for Scouting was reined in, as guidance from Headquarters advised Guides not to parade in public or try to ape the activities of the boys (which was what had interested them in the movement in the first place). It was also suggested that they camp indoors to begin with, as it was felt the outdoor life might be harmful to their delicate health. There is evidence to suggest that these new directions were a great disappointment to the groups of girls who had already been inspired to form their own troops and had based their activities around the instructions in *Scouting For Boys*. Rose Kerr, an early Guide leader who has also written a history of the movement, has suggested that 'many felt that the scheme now proposed for them, with its substitution of nursing and domestic duties for the more boyish activities, was rather a watered-down edition of Scouting'.[61]

Indeed, the memories of other early Guides suggest that it was just those 'boyish' activities that they most enjoyed. In those pre-war days when the adult press and juvenile literature were filled with stories about the threat of invasion and the likelihood of war, Girl Scout troops appeared to be ignoring Baden-Powell's advice and preparing themselves for battle. Miss Raschen, who was captain of the 1st Birkenhead troop, remembers the early days of the movement:

> We wore Lincoln green dresses with red ties and red tam-o-shanters in winter, and white straw hats with green bands round them for summer. Lieutenants, leaders, and corporals wore white chevrons on the arm, like the N.C.O.s in the army. We always wore a white haversack filled to overflowing with first-aid requisites, and carried a cloth-covered water bottle slung on the shoulder. And last but not least, we never moved without our poles! Then of course we had our band (perish the thought!) complete with drums and bugles – oh yes the town knew when the Guides went out in those days![62]

Groups at grass roots level, it seems, took little notice of the entreaties to 'ladylike' behaviour; they adopted uniforms and even had military ranks, something the Boy Scouts themselves did not have. Another early Girl Guide from Devon remembers feeling similarly excited by the idea of action:

> We had nobody to help us, but we felt immensely patriotic and – whisper it low – distinctly martial in spirit. This may have been due partly to the thrill of evolving a uniform, and the courage it took to walk along the street in it when we had evolved it![63]

Courage was definitely needed to march down the street in uniform, as public sympathy for the Guides was initially extremely low. Baden-Powell was right; polite society, and even impolite society, didn't want to see women parading in the streets, carrying rucksacks and wooden poles, attempting to train themselves to be useful in time of crisis. Miss Stockdale, who commanded a troop of girls in Liverpool, recalls having all sorts of things thrown at them when they marched down the street in 1909. Then again, it is hardly likely that that would have upset her girls, as they were a tough lot:

> When the girls got at loggerheads with each other we made them put on boxing gloves and settle their differences in cold blood. This really was very effective and stopped tale bearing.[64]

Similarly unladylike activities were sometimes actively concealed from Scouting and Guiding headquarters. The girls at Lingholt boarding school in Hindhead, for example, formed two rival troops, the Night-Hawks and the Wild Cats, and waged a constant war against each other, each determining to steal as much of the other troop's equipment as possible:

> This thrilling life lasted for over a year, during which we gained many badges. But alas, Boy Scout headquarters finally discovered that we were girls, and demanded the return of our badges! (We had obtained them by the device of giving our initials only, not our Christian names, when applying)

> Then came the day of change. The Games Mistress was appointed captain; the beloved Night-Hawks had to become the Heather patrol, and the Wild Cats descended to being Bracken.[65]

This change of troops' names from animals to flowers seems to have upset many Girl Scout troops who had initially named themselves, as the boys did, after animals. Miss G. N. Commander of the 1st Birmingham company remembers:

> We very reluctantly changed from being Scouts to Guides ... It seemed rather a come down to be flowers instead of animals, and the ideal of womanliness had no appeal for us at that age.[66]

The constant emphasis throughout early Guide literature on the idea of womanliness closely associated with that of motherhood, Tammy

Proctor has suggested, was a response to the struggle for women's suf-
frage. The Guide Association had to walk a thin line between the
conservative forces of domestic or maternal respectability and feminist forces seeking new opportunities for girls to participate in society.
Anti-suffragists feared that emancipated women would neglect their
home and family, and so it was important, if the Guides were to gain
public support, that their movement be associated with the nurturing,
home-loving modern woman. Proctor goes further:

> Girl Guides had to be womanly in order to answer adult anxi-
> eties about new freedoms for females. Guides were taught to be
> sympathetic and trained in home skills, and also they were taught
> to desire the company of men. Leaders thought that girls should
> become wives, not independent women. Some wanted to train girls
> to become 'companions' for men, but not equals; they wanted to save
> girls from depravity and moral disintegration, so that as women they,
> in turn, could save men.[67]

What the accounts of local Guide groups suggest, however, is that the
girls themselves had little interest in being trained as 'companions'
for men. That is not why they set themselves up as Girl Scouts, and
they initially resisted the new training suggested for them. They had
become interested, like the boys who became Scouts, in the outdoor
life. They saw opportunities for adventure in learning signalling, tracking and camping skills. They wanted uniforms, a band, the chance for
action, and, when left to themselves, that is what they did. Clearly
some of their early troop leaders, probably little more than girls themselves, also wanted these things for their girls. They organised the
marches and bands and even promoted boxing for girls as a way to
settle disputes. It seems likely that it was only as the Guide Association's central organising authority grew that it was able to insist on
having groups led by approved leaders, following the guidelines laid
out in *The Handbook for Girl Guides*. Even then, in the early years local
groups adapted the rules to suit their membership and their interests,
and many girls continued to enjoy the more 'boyish' elements allowed
in the training.

Guiding in wartime

With the outbreak of war, however, the Guide movement adapted itself
quickly to the new demands on the civilian population, and the old

concerns with respectability and motherhood training were superseded by the new concerns for better-trained women to serve in auxiliary capacities. Partially responsible for this new direction was the input the Guides began to receive from Baden-Powell's young wife in 1914. Olave Soames was just 23 when she married the 55-year-old Chief Scout in 1912, and in 1914 she began to take an active interest in the Guide movement. Olave was made Chief Commissioner in October 1914, and in that year began a series of letters to the *Girl Guide Gazette* – a magazine for both girls and their leaders. The Association was keen to explain to its girls how the Guide teachings on self-sacrifice and serving others could be practised in the face of war. Olave's letter to the Guides that opened the August 1914 edition of the *Girl Guide Gazette* explained that, while men were being asked to sacrifice their lives, so women must try hard to make sacrifices and help others. She advised that girls should concentrate on cheering those who were obliged to part, visiting their homes and offering to care for their children or help look after the housework. Most importantly, one of their chief duties was to maintain discipline, as no work could be achieved without order, discipline and obedience. She writes:

> Prompt obedience to orders is what every soldier has to learn, and it is instant, cheerful obedience which helps to make everything go smoothly.[68]

While rejoicing that older Guides trained in first aid would have the opportunity to become VADs (Voluntary Aid Detachment nurses), Olave Baden-Powell stressed that younger Guides should continue their first aid and ambulance training as well as offering their services to local army camps to help cook and clean, distribute books and magazines, and knit and make clothes.

As the war progressed, the girls' attentions were also drawn to the plight of their brother Scouts. Many, it was pointed out, were doing the country a valuable service by keeping watch over bridges, telegraph lines and reservoirs as well as the huge task of keeping watch over the coastline in the place of the coastguards, who had been called up into the Navy. The girls, it was advised, could do no greater service than knitting warm clothes for these brave boys who were sure to be spending many cold nights out in the open.

Across the country girls were sewing and knitting for soldiers, volunteering in hospitals, making bandages and splints, acting as messengers and helping with postal deliveries; in fact, offering themselves to any local body that could use their help. In Edinburgh, a Guide in the 7th company remembers:

> We went every Saturday morning in 1917 to run messages between the depot in Lauriston Place and the Red Cross Stall in the Princes Street Arcade where home-made marmalade was sold for the war effort. We visited the junk shops to collect empty jam jars which we wheeled about in an empty pram. Not very glamorous, but we felt we were helping to win the war – nothing else would have persuaded us to wheel an old pram filled with dirty jam jars.[69]

Additionally, Robert Baden-Powell wrote to the *Girl Guide Gazette* suggesting that the Guides transform their clubrooms into temporary hostels that could be used as shelters or makeshift hospitals in the case of bombing raids or invasion by the enemy. In a letter to the magazine in October 1915, Baden-Powell wrote of the great work being done by women in France and urged the Guides to 'Be Prepared' for their chance to do great deeds for their country. He wrote: 'The Zeppelins – bless them! – will be a great help to you in this way', and entreated the girls to 'be prepared for casualties anywhere women and children are gathered'. [70] His letter went on:

> You know what I mean. Have you got your hostels ready for taking in those injured or rendered homeless by bombardment? Have you your stretchers and bandages ready? Have you learnt to bind up wounds and put out fires? Have you learnt to keep your head and to be plucky in a panic? Have you determined to think nothing of your own safety and to sacrifice it if needs be in order to save others, as these other heroines have done?[71]

Girls who did this were to be considered 'real Guides', and it seems likely that such an entreaty would have left many Guide troops desperate for some casualties to whisk off to their makeshift hospital beds to demonstrate their bandage-tying prowess – if they endangered their own lives in the course of the rescue, so much the better.

While Baden-Powell and the Guide Association recognised the new and varied opportunities the war provided for girls to gain some practical experience of what the training was aiming to instil in them, it was still important that they kept their sense of place and decency. Appeals were made to ensure that uniform regulations were strictly adhered to and that no added decoration should creep in, and on one

Figure 4.2   Girl Guides with a stretcher and other equipment in preparation for post-air raid emergency help
Source: Imperial War Museum.

occasion Baden-Powell wrote to the *Gazette* deploring the conduct of a group of Guides who had dressed in band uniforms and given a public concert. It was always pointed out that the men at the Front did not appreciate women behaving 'in a hysterical way', donning uniforms and adopting a pseudo-militaristic demeanour. In May 1915, in another of his monthly letters to the *Gazette*, Baden-Powell wrote of his pleasure on hearing that Girl Guides in some centres, when asked to parade with public recruiting processions, had declined, not feeling it was the right place for them. He extolled their virtues, saying how glad they were to do useful work 'behind the scenes', in offices and factories and in the homes of soldiers' wives and children. Emphatically, he said:

> Men are not going to be persuaded to enlist because a lot of children go about the streets waving flags; but it is entirely another matter when they see everybody, including even the girls of the nation, seriously at work doing their bit towards the defence of the Empire, and for the successful issue to the war.[72]

The first Annual Report of the Girl Guides was for the year 1916, a year in which the association had received something of a revamp, with a new organisational structure for the counties and increasing input from Robert Baden-Powell himself. The report is clear about the significance of the war for the place of women in society and the way in which it was believed it helped encourage public acceptance of the Girl Guides as a movement:

> The War has brought to women their opportunity. It has shown how they are needed in the work of the world; it has shown how they are capable if trained aright; it has shown how, through misdirection of education, they have been handicapped in the past.[73]

The education women needed to prepare them for their place in the world is described as being that of gaining efficiency through character, skill and health, and particularly, for poorer women, in encouraging improvements in environment, handicrafts, homecrafts and hygiene. Guiding had been established to these ends, and through the war the practical implications of this training had been particularly brought home to both the girls and society at large. Without the war it was felt that it would have taken a long time to persuade suspicious parents, the public and educationalists that the movement was not just a factory for 'Tom-boys'. The war had broken down old traditions and prejudices and shown the value of service given by women if properly trained.

By 1916 some 50,000 girls had enrolled as Guides, and 2,450 Brownies had joined the junior branch (begun in 1915 to cater for girls between 8 and 11). During the course of the war so far, Guides had turned their clubrooms into hostels, acted as messengers in government departments, made garments and bandages, and worked cooking and cleaning in hospitals. In addition, they had raised £2,000 for recreation huts for soldiers in France, through fund-raising activities, not through soliciting donations, something both the Guide and Scout Associations considered to be begging, and not at all in the spirit of their teachings on self-reliance and initiative. Work of this kind meant that, by 1916, 3,753 War Service Badges had been awarded to Guides for such duties.

In 1917 Olave Baden-Powell rewrote the Guide handbook, changing its name to *Training Girls as Guides*. Having never got along with her husband's sister, Olave was keen to remove Agnes from the leadership of the Guides and took over the position of Chief Guide herself in 1917. The new handbook didn't differ particularly in tone; it stressed the importance of learning mothering skills and the need for true womanliness to repair the damage caused by war and to return the country to a stable social footing. What was different was the emphasis placed on self-control and patriotism. The need now was for 'citizen mothers', girls trained to be efficient, yet womanly, nurturers of the coming generations.[74] The appeal was to the adventurous, responsible girl who saw the importance of her future role and accepted it.[75] According to Tammy Proctor:

> Looking fearfully to the threat from within – the new woman – and the threat from without – bolshevism – Olave Baden-Powell promoted the Guides as directing girls' energy in a positive, constructive direction.[76]

But it wasn't only the feminist 'new woman' that Olave hoped Guiding would curb. Guiding could also be used to help rein in that other female threat to the social order, the 'flapper'.[77] Young wartime women, taking advantage of their new-found freedoms and increased spending power, were perceived to be behaving in more and more inappropriate ways, wearing make-up and expensive clothes, smoking cigarettes and eating out alone in public.[78] These girls were particularly likely to fall victim to that other wartime affliction – 'khaki fever' – and find themselves unable to resist any young man in uniform. This was considered a serious threat to the health of the armed forces, through the spread of venereal disease, as well as to the moral fibre of the nation.[79] Shortly before a huge Girl Guide rally in Hyde Park in 1918, Olave Baden-Powell gave an interview to the *Daily Mirror* which they reported in an article entitled 'Is the end of the flighty Flapper's day in sight?' In it she claimed the Guides:

> Enrol flappers – if I may call the young girls so – of every kind and aim at making them women of character. Every class joins, every type, and they turn out clear-headed, happy women of trained character.[80]

Lady Baden-Powell felt that the prime aim of the movement was to provide wholesome occupation for girls in their spare time and so divert their minds from more 'undesirable' things. Girls no longer had the same love of home that the older generation considered so important; instead, she believed, 'the girls wanted to be out and about, they had the war fever on them'.[81] What girls needed was a movement that was going to direct their energies away from the streets and the soldiers and back into the home. By encouraging them to work for the war, but in primarily domestic tasks, girls could be persuaded to join and then have their enthusiasm channelled back into appropriate womanly and modest activities.

Guiding's role was to train future citizens, and that role took on an even greater significance during wartime, as the country began to recognise the important part the next generation was going to play in rebuilding the country after the war was over. Just as we will see with the education debate, those involved in Guide leadership began to stress the fact that the war would not necessarily end when the fighting was over. Britain would have to continue to fight, in trade and commerce, to maintain its position as leader of a great empire. To that end it was felt that:

> The Munitions which we have to get ready for this coming war are the men and women of the next generation, upon whom will fall the brunt of the struggle.[82]

This was why Guide training was so important. It was believed that the inefficiencies of the pre-war years, characterised by high infant mortality due to preventable disease, could be eliminated by efficient, well-trained mothers of the future, proficient in homecraft and hygiene.[83] Therefore Guiding:

> offers to women of every standing a glorious and ready opportunity of doing that for their country of which perhaps they had never dreamed before that they were capable – a bigger and more permanent work even than the present war work because it affects the coming generation, and will help to maintain what we shall have won in the present War, and to compensate in some degree for our enormous sacrifices of blood and treasure.[84]

While the war had shown Guides, and women in general, new and more exciting opportunities for work and activities outside the home, it was still presumed that most women would return to their pre-war lives, thus making Guiding's motherhood training all the more relevant. These girls were vital to Britain's post-war reconstruction – they were needed to help rebuild Britain, but as mothers, not as workers. If they were to be confined to the domestic sphere, at least, as Allen Warren has said, their preparation for that role 'had become more diverse and less inevitable'.[85] The Guide Association built on the success of the war years, and the interest in their movement that it generated, and no doubt girls continued to be interested in the movement because of the element of personal freedom and independence that participation offered to them. From 50,000 members in 1916, the Guides had a membership of 120,000 in England by 1919, and during the 1920s their membership exceeded that of their brother Boy Scouts.[86]

Undoubtedly the war helped the growth and development of Guiding, as many girls must have joined because of the opportunities it afforded them for feeling that they were 'doing their bit' for their country in its time of need. The Association saw that enthusiasm for the movement might die down after the war, but felt that the new demands of reconstruction, with the promise of increased opportunities for well-trained girls, would help the Guides to continue growing. Most of all it was felt that the war had been a test, a test of the training offered by the scheme and of the work that could be achieved by well-trained girls and women. They had passed that test, and in some ways the war had validated their principles and the reasoning behind the programme. Britain's power and position in the world were under threat, and it would take a concerted effort on the part of all citizens to hold off that threat in the future. The training of both boys and girls was seen to be central to that end, and, as the war had shown, such training could produce young people both willing and able to jump to their country's call.

5

War in the Classroom

As the First World War drew to a close and the country began to reflect on the extent of its losses, attention turned to the future and the means by which the nation could rebuild itself. H.A.L. Fisher, President of the Board of Education promoting the 1918 Education Act, said:

> I conceive that it is part of the duty of our generation to provide some means for compensating the tragic loss which our nation is enduring, and that one means by which some compensation may be provided is by the creation of a system of education throughout the country which will increase the value of every human unit in the whole of society.[1]

Just as they had been after the disastrous South African Wars, children were seen as the natural resource that promised hope to the injured empire. It was through education that the Reconstruction Committee of the Coalition government felt that hope could best be realised. The war had revealed dangerous limitations to the school curriculum, with Britain lagging behind her German rivals in the fields of science and technology, and there was concern that so many children had been driven out of school and into industry to meet the demands of the wartime economy. During the war these concerns informed the education debate, and reformers sought to use these new issues to build on pre-war interest in educational psychology and teaching methods to inspire an Education Act that would cater for both the needs of the child and the needs of the economy.

But what was happening in schools? This chapter will consider the impact of the war on the daily lives of children and their teachers at work in the nation's classrooms. Schools had an important role in protecting their pupils both physically and psychologically from the dangers of war, and this chapter will explore the ways in which schools and teachers tried to minimise the threats to their pupils' safety. It will also consider how the war entered the curriculum to inform lessons on history, geography and citizenship. The war proved how important it was for the population to be willing and prepared to fight and work for the empire's survival, and it was increasingly felt that much of that preparation should be done in schools. Children were mobilised for the war effort as a way of teaching them the value of participating in a national endeavour. They could learn important lessons on citizenship by being citizens, collecting, saving and making things for the war effort.

The nature and structure of public education in Edwardian Britain were undergoing some significant changes in the pre-war years, and the types of schools and the age to which children attended varied widely throughout the country. In general, elementary schools catered for children from the age of 5 up to, but not necessarily until, 14. The schools were arranged in Standards, I–VI, through which the children progressed as they reached the required level of attainment. There was no uniform school leaving age, with children in some areas being allowed to leave as early as 11 and others not until 12 or 13. For those seeking post-elementary education there were fewer opportunities within the state sector, and again the provision varied widely. For those who could afford it, there were fee-paying grammar schools that offered a general curriculum carrying on from the subjects studied at elementary level, but these were beyond the means of most working-class parents. Alternatively, in some areas, predominantly the industrial centres of London and Manchester, there were the emerging higher-grade schools and Commercial and Technical Schools, which sought to provide a more vocational curriculum for children intending to enter industry or commerce at age 16.

Elementary education in Britain had been transformed since the end of the nineteenth century by a number of factors that had promoted a new understanding of both the role of the teacher and the purpose of education. The end, in 1895, of the system of 'payment by results', whereby school funding and teachers' salaries had depended on the performance of their children in a narrow range of examined subjects, allowed a broadening of the curriculum from its narrow focus on the 'three Rs' to include the humanities and sciences as well as drawing and handiwork.[2] In addition, the progressive influence of educational psychology gained ground amongst ordinary teachers, and the theories of pioneers like Friedrich Froebel and Johann Heinrich Pestalozzi led to the gradual rise of the child-centred approach to education.[3]

In 1902 the Balfour Education Act replaced the existing 3,000 or so ad hoc school boards and school attendance committees with 318 Local Education Authorities having responsibility for all forms of State education within their area. The LEAs were under the control of the Board of Education, which issued a new set of Regulations for Elementary Schools in 1904, conveying the sense of the new liberal and purposeful thinking on education:

> The purpose of the Public Elementary School is to form and strengthen the character and to develop the intelligence of the children entrusted to it, and to make the best use of the school years available, in assisting both girls and boys, according to their different needs, to fit themselves, practically as well as intellectually, for the work of life.[4]

This marked a clear departure from the emphasis on mechanical rote learning of the previous century, as well as an acknowledgement of the role of the school in developing individual children, not merely keeping them off the streets until they were old enough to enter employment. Even more constructive was the advice given in the handbook of *Suggestions for the Consideration of Teachers and Others concerned with the Work of Public Elementary Schools*, published in 1905 by the Board of Education. The *Suggestions* are considered a landmark both in the official acknowledgement of a more child-centred approach to education and in the State's recognition of a more independent role for the elementary teacher.[5] They advised that:

> The teacher must know the children and must sympathise with them, for it is of the essence of teaching that the mind of the teachers should touch the mind of the pupil ... and though the teachers can influence only a short period of the lives of the scholars, yet it is the period where human nature is most plastic, when good influence is most fruitful.[6]

Secondary education was slower to benefit from the progressive attitude towards elementary education fostered by the 1902 Balfour Act. Initially the Act put an end to the Higher Grade elementary schools, begun by some school boards, which allowed the further education of elementary school children past Standard VI. The intention of the classically educated administrators, such as Robert Morant, Permanent Secretary at the Board of Education (1903–1911), was to maintain the emphasis on classical education in secondary schools, in essence reserving post-elementary education for the children of the middle and upper classes. There was little encouragement from the Board for the technical and vocational subjects designed to meet the needs of pupils entering industry at 16, offered by the new junior technical schools and central schools of London and Manchester.[7]

However, some moves were made to increase access to secondary education, and in 1907 the Liberal government, in response to demands from labour groups and trade unions, introduced a major free-place scheme to grant-aided secondary schools. Under the scheme, up to one-quarter of the pupil intake was to come from elementary school pupils who passed the qualifying examination. By 1911, over 82,000 former elementary school pupils were at secondary school, about 60 per cent of the total intake, and roughly a third of them received free education.[8] For the mass of the population, however, there were still few opportunities for secondary education. By the beginning of the First World War, of every 1,000 pupils aged between 10 and 11 attending elementary schools, only 56 went on to a secondary education. This situation has led the historian, Brian Simon, to conclude that the odds against such children receiving a secondary education stood at 40 to 1.[9]

Newspaper coverage of the new educational theories and a growing awareness amongst labour groups of the significance of educational provision led to increased calls for further reforms to education immediately before the war, including an extension of the school leaving age, a broader curriculum and an increase in the scholarship funds available for children to progress on to secondary education and beyond. Educationalists' calls for an increase in the school leaving age to 14 without exception came in part from the inconsistencies under the existing law, allowing children in different areas to leave school as early as 11, but in other areas not until 12 or 13. This confusion was compounded by the continuing practice of the half-time system, whereby children attended school for half the day and then went to work for the other half of the day. This system was mainly found in Yorkshire and Lancashire, where children were employed in the textile industries and as agricultural labourers. By 1914–1915, the Board of Education estimated that there were 69,555 half-timers in England and Wales.[10] In addition to extending the school leaving age to 14, LEAs were calling for the introduction of continuation schools, where children who left school at 14 would attend for a set number of hours per year until they were 18.

Continuation schools were designed to combat the growing problem of adolescents who left school and entered 'blind alley' occupations where they were employed on relatively high wages for a couple of years, before being fired and replaced by another school leaver. It was felt that these young people, predominantly boys, were escaping the reforming influence of both school and serious employment, and, after losing their jobs, were likely to become delinquent. This attention to the plight of the adolescent was in keeping with the social reforms of the Liberal government and the concerns of the Imperialist lobby. Both sought to remedy the perceived deficiencies in the health and moral well being of the population following the evidence provided by the 1904 Committee on Physical Deterioration which was set up after the Boer War. The next ten years saw the issue of Britain's strength and 'national efficiency' constantly connected to the condition of her future citizens. Children were seen as both the hope and the downfall of the British Empire, and, as discussed in the previous chapter, all sorts of movements developed with an interest in shaping the future leaders and soldiers of the empire.

The declaration of war in August 1914 forced aside plans for a new Education Bill in 1914. Instead, education authorities were faced with new problems related to the staffing of schools and the attendance of pupils. By mid-1916 over 20,000 male elementary teachers, approximately half the pre-war numbers, had left their posts to join the army, and the number of male students in the teacher training colleges had also declined dramatically. This shortfall was partially overcome by the employment of women teachers in boys' departments. Approximately 17,500 women had replaced men on military service by 1916.[11] Many women teachers sought to obtain leave of absence in order to serve in nursing units or in the women's auxiliary services, prompting the Board of Education to issue statements calling on women teachers to serve their country in the schools rather than on the battlefields.[12] If the schools were able to make up for the shortage of numbers caused by male teachers enlisting in the first two years of the war, they found their situation unworkable after conscription was introduced. At this point the army allowed teachers of a low medical category on Home Service to resume their teaching duties, and also agreed that certain teachers and education officials might be reserved from service.

Another serious effect of the war on children's education came from the relaxation of the school attendance by-laws, which, from as early as August 1914, allowed children to leave school to go to work in industries suffering labour shortages because of the war. This problem was particularly acute in agricultural areas, where farmers, unwilling to employ women or to increase adult wages, found children a cheap source of labour at harvest and sowing time. By 1916 15,753 children, mostly boys, had been exempted from school to become agricultural labourers. Of those children, 546 were aged between 11 and 12.[13] As the war went on, the problem increased. More and more children were exempted from school to work on the land and in industry. Overall, the numbers leaving elementary school between the ages of 12 and 14 increased from 196,943 in 1915 to 240,556 by 1917.[14]

Added to this problem was the significant shift in patterns of employment amongst school leavers. The high wages on offer in the wartime industries meant there was a rapid move away from peacetime occupations which offered a greater possibility of a lasting career. By October 1916 approximately 205,000 boys and girls were employed in the manufacture of munitions.[15] At Woolwich Arsenal alone there were 10,000 boys, of whom 3,000 were aged between 14 and 16, working shifts up to 12 hours long.[16] This situation echoed the pre-war issue of 'blind-alley' employment that had first prompted the need for the proposed continuation schools. During the war educationalists were increasingly concerned about these children, who, they felt, were being sacrificed to the needs of the war. These concerns led to the setting up of the Departmental Committee on Juvenile Education in Relation to Employment after the War. The committee recommended that teachers should encourage children and their parents that staying in full-time education was a better option than joining the labour market just at the time when demobilised soldiers were returning.

Despite these problems, the Board of Education mobilised the nation's children both mentally and physically throughout the war, introducing the war into the curriculum and inciting the children to contribute both their time and money towards its successful prosecution. With the whole country mobilised to support the war effort through drives to raise money, conserve food and serve in auxiliary services, the government, through the Board of Education, recognised the unique opportunity it had to transmit its message into British homes though school children. If organised appropriately by the schools, children could be put to work for the war effort and, through their involvement, influence their parents. Not only would the children's own activities contribute towards the war effort, but the example of best practice demonstrated by the school would find its way into the nation's homes. The schools became an agency for the dissemination of all sorts of pieces of advice to the public during the war, from how to cook economically to how to convert back gardens into allotments.

In 1916 the Board of Education was asked by the Board of Agriculture and Fisheries to issue a circular to public elementary schools about the food supply, suggesting ways in which children and schools could help increase national food production. They recognised the difficult circumstances under which schools were operating, but felt confident that:

> every Elementary School which is in a position to do so will be ready to assist at the present time in any work which can contribute directly or indirectly to the national welfare.[17]

The circular then listed the ways in which schools were already helping in terms of food production, mentioning gardening, the keeping of animals and, for girls, the making of jam and the preserving of fruits and vegetables. In mentioning gardening, the circular says:

> In October 1915 there were 3,129 school gardens in England in which 56,037 children of Elementary School age were receiving instruction in practical gardening. Efforts will no doubt be made, by intensive cultivation and a well arranged system of secondary cropping, to use every yard of land in these gardens to the best advantage throughout the year.[18]

The Board suggested that to do this schools should attempt to acquire more land, making use of derelict or unused plots, and also proposed that gardening classes could take over the cultivation of the gardens belonging to men in the Forces or those otherwise engaged in war work. Going even further, it proposed that schools become centres for seed testing and use their influence to facilitate the co-operation of local farmers in the lending of expensive equipment. This suggested a new role for the school, not only as a purveyor of advice, but also as a central organising authority for war work at a local level. Whether any school succeeded in running such a scheme is unclear, although there is no reason why enterprising teachers, keen to contribute more than just their teaching abilities, would not have been able to organise something of this sort.

The Board had already issued a pamphlet to teachers of domestic science, explaining the need for increased economy in the preparation of food, and charging them with spreading this message into homes through their pupils. Now they supplemented this with a call for more

Figure 5.1 Schoolgirls with the produce of their school 1914
Source: Imperial War Museum.

attention to be paid to the cooking of vegetables rather than meat, and added that:

> More time might also be given to those branches of domestic work which in large households come within the province of the still-room maid but which are equally within reach of the clever cottage house-wife.[19]

Here they suggest the girls should be trained in jam making, the bottling and drying of fruit, and pickle and chutney making. The teaching of domestic subjects to girls gained more urgency during the war as the number of women entering domestic service declined in favour of jobs in the service industries and industry which offered better pay and conditions.[20] But the thought expressed here, that girls might also make use of these skills in their own homes, rather than while in service, also reflects contemporary concerns over the future role of these girls as wives and mothers. The huge loss of life on the battlefield and the enormous social dislocation on the home front often led to strong reactionary attitudes that urged women back into the home to take care of their husbands and children. Despite the new opportunities for women to work outside the home opening up during the war, the Board of Education remained content with steering girls towards work in traditional fields.

Where teachers were experienced animal keepers, the Board urged them to pass on their knowledge to the pupils and to keep animals at school. Chickens could be kept for both eggs and meat, and it was also suggested that children might learn how to manage an incubator and to foster-mother chicks. Rabbits were also proposed as suitable animals for schools to keep, although a market would need to be found for them in neighbouring villages, as local prejudice was likely to prevent the use of tame rabbits for food in places where wild rabbits were plentiful.[21] Even very young children could help, harvesting wild plants and fruit from fields and hedgerows.

Despite all this good work that children could do, the Board of Education was at pains to remind teachers of the importance of discipline when it came to the children's work. They warned:

a) Teachers will need to impress strongly on the children the importance of getting through the outdoor work of the school in reasonable time. If children are allowed to loiter and 'make a job last out' in order to escape indoor lessons, they will quickly acquire bad habits of indolence and more harm than good will result.

b) All practical work should be marked by scrupulous order, neatness and cleanliness. Tools and utensils of all kinds should be cleaned every time they are used before putting them away in their proper places.[22]

Instilling a sense of order and discipline in their pupils was seen as just as important a task for teachers as imparting knowledge. Education and the work of the schools was seen as a reforming influence on working-class children, brought up, it was believed, with poor discipline and few morals. By coming into contact with the superior manners and behaviour of their teachers in the schools, it was felt these children could be reformed, and that they in turn could influence their parents at home. Discipline was key if the children were to develop into good, diligent workers. The schools intended working-class children, to become hardworking, obedient employees, learning their place in society while at school through strict discipline and few opportunities for independent action.

War in the curriculum

> No body can escape from the war feeling, which is in the very air ... It would be absurd to endeavour to escape from this, and

to try to immerse oneself in a calm philosophy, for it could not
be done. The boys at school, above all, could not do it, nor
even the girls, and the effect of the war feeling upon them is
inevitable; it must, therefore, be reckoned with, for it will affect
them not only now but, maybe, for the whole of their lives.[23]

The Schoolmaster – October 1914

As soon as war broke out, both teachers and schools were asking for
guidance as to what should be taught about the war, recognising both
the undeniable interest of their pupils as well as the unique opportunity the war represented for breathing new life into the existing
curriculum. Over the following four years the war informed teaching
on everything from history and geography to English and lessons on
citizenship. The desire was to invoke the spirit of patriotism and give
children a sense of national identity and their place at the heart of a
great empire under threat. To do this, tales of past and present heroes
were told alongside lessons on the geography of Europe and the economic and social history of the combatant nations. As for the children,
there is evidence from inspection reports that their attention and interest in schoolwork improved. Teachers were able to connect their lessons
to the events of the world outside, to which so many of the children
had a personal connection, with fathers and brothers serving in the
forces.

The aim was for children to be taught to understand that Britain's
participation in the war was not only right, but that it was part of the
history of a great nation, of which the children were an integral part.
An article in *The Schoolmaster*, the weekly newspaper of the National
Union of Teachers (NUT), urged teachers to recognise this:

The claims and the beauty of patriotism must be kept in mind, the
glory of our country sharing gallantly and effectively in a just and
needful war must be dwelt on, and nothing must be done or said
which might weaken a child's sense that he is one of a great company
of people, a member of a race which, in the present as in the past,
has shown its fitness to gain, occupy, and hold a great international
position for the benefit of the whole world as well as for ourselves.[24]

Concerns over national efficiency had led to a wave of legislation to
protect and promote the health and well being of children in order
to safeguard the empire – now it was time for the children to understand why. Unlike past lessons, on far away places involving people the
children had little in common with, this war provided teachers with

the opportunity of showing the children how ordinary Britons, their fathers and brothers, were displaying all the qualities of patriotism and self-sacrifice that had made the British Empire great.

But the article went on to urge teachers to impress upon their pupils that war in itself is 'no gain, no permanent and biological necessity'. Should they fail to make this clear, the teachers would be falling into the trap their German counterparts had in recent years, educating the nation's children to glorify war and strive for national expansion. It was the responsibility of teachers to 'try to make war on future war by our teaching as soon as this war is done'.[25]

So this was no rampant jingoism; at the core, these lessons were intended to be educational. Teachers were genuinely looking for ways to harness the children's newfound interest in world affairs to teach them something of their country's history and national character. The enthusiasm with which individual teachers and the Board of Education responded to the demands of the children for lessons on the war can be seen as a result of the new thinking on child-centred teaching methods that had been growing in the years before the war.

Children at state elementary schools in Britain just before and during the war studied a curriculum broadly outlined by the Board of Education. *The 1905 Suggestions for the Consideration of Teachers and Others Concerned in the Work of the Public Elementary Schools* had chapters devoted to English, Arithmetic, Observation Lessons and Nature Study, Geography, History, Drawing, Singing, Physical Training, Needlework and Housecraft (for girls) and Handicraft and Gardening (for boys). However, these were, as the title of the publication explains, suggestions, and there was no prescribed syllabus or core texts to be studied in all schools. Indeed, the *Suggestions* were keen to point out that:

> The only uniformity of practice that the Board of Education desire to see in the teaching of Public Elementary Schools is that each teacher shall think for himself and work out for himself such methods of teaching as may use his powers to the best advantage and be best suited to the particular needs and conditions of the school.[26]

The curriculum of state post-elementary schools varied depending on the type of institution. Junior technical and industrial schools were developing in the early years of the century, focusing on a range of subjects from manual and scientific to clerical subjects, designed to prepare adolescents leaving school at 16. Grammar and grant-aided secondary schools concentrated on a more academic curriculum, in essence carried on from the subjects studied at elementary school level.

In light of the demands from teachers and schools for specific guidance on how to incorporate the war into the existing school curriculum, the Board of Education issued a circular suggesting a course in history for the higher forms in schools to give a background to the war.

Modern European history was to include German history, concentrating on the country's unification, the liberation of Italy, including the achievements of Garibaldi, the gradual disintegration of the Ottoman Empire and the establishment of independent Christian states in Eastern Europe, as well as Russian and Austrian history. The basic principles of the course were to give a general outline of the political history as well as to present the outstanding events, episodes and personalities of the period. The Board also stressed that use should be made of the children's foreign language skills, encouraging teachers to use French and German texts on the Napoleonic Wars as well as English ones. Just as we saw in the *Schoolmaster* article, the Board of Education made it clear to teachers that the course should be as intellectually balanced as possible so as not to 'encourage national animosities'.[27]

The teaching of history was to become not only a lesson in the past strength of a great empire but also an example for the future. British military heroes from Nelson to General Gordon were held up for emulation by teachers keen to give their children, and boys in particular, examples of the characteristics considered great and essential in a time of war – courage, fortitude, sacrifice and honour amongst them. Ideal British characteristics were also extolled when attempts were made to explain the causes of war to children. The Board of Education would occasionally recommend particular commercially produced war-themed texts for use in schools, including *Why Britain Went to War – To the Boys and Girls of the British Empire*. Written by Sir James Yoxall, MP and secretary of the NUT, the text uses the playground analogy to explain Britain's position to children:

> In all this war there is nothing for us to be ashamed of: we fight for honour. You know what honour is among schoolboys – I do not mean prize-winning, or getting one's name written in gold letters upon an honours board, but straight dealing, truth-speaking, and 'playing the game'. Well *we* are standing up for honour among nations while Germany is playing the sneak and the bully in the big European school. Germany must be taught to 'play cricket', to play fair, to

honour a 'scrap of paper', not to be false or cruel, and not to threaten and brag. A boy who behaved as Germany has done would be 'sent to Coventry' by all the school.[28]

Albert A Cock's *A Syllabus in War Geography and History*, published in 1916, takes a more sophisticated view on the causes of war in the final chapter of his book, entitled 'Ethical Questions'. The chapter contains suggestions for teachers about how to explain the necessity of the war to children, stating:

> Economic and ethical problems are always closely intertwined, and the intelligent pupil will probably be stirred to raise the question of the morality of the attack upon Belgium, and perhaps the morality of 'crushing Germany'.[29]

To explain these questions to children, Cock believed it important to approach the matter in other ways than by solely insisting on the sacredness of treaty obligations. He says:

> Let us think of the problem in terms of personality. We may legit-imately conceive of a nation as having, in its corporate life, a personality of its own. As such, it is entitled to the respect and to the independence which attach to the status of being a *person*. This is a right inalienable by any treaty. It can never cease to be a right. At all times and in all places, personhood is sacred and inviolable: to respect it is one formulation of the Kantian categorical imperative.[30]

Perhaps this difference in tone can be explained by the fact that Cock is writing two years later, when much of the initial enthusiasm for the war has begun to be replaced by a grim acceptance of the likelihood of a protracted struggle. Instead of a simplistic appeal to children's sense of right and wrong, Cock recognises that some pupils are likely to be questioning the validity of their earlier belief in the justification for war. What he does is to urge the children to think about the problem from a philosophical perspective and to understand that the issues transcend the bounds of the existing crisis.

Despite this more sophisticated approach, there were still many in 1916 who saw the opportunity the war provided for inculcating into children more particular lessons in patriotism and self-sacrifice. Richard Wilson, in his *The First Year of the Great War*, published in 1916, also explained Britain's position in terms of teaching Germany to 'play fair' but then went on to discuss the personal lessons children might learn from the war:

> I hope to show you some of the bright-eyed heroism of the noble sons of Britain, among whom some of your own friends, brothers, cousins were doubtless numbered. If you who read this book can lay claim to one who gave up his life in the war, then you have a splendid pattern before you for the rest of your life; and you now know something of the true meaning of those noble words. 'Greater love hath no man than this, that a man lay down his life for his friends'.[31]

This lesson of personal sacrifice for the common good was so important that many felt the learning of it should not be left to chance. A debate on the teaching of patriotism in schools was held in the House of Lords in November 1915, where speakers stressed the importance of impressing upon children a true sense of patriotism and the duties of citizenship. During the debate Lord Sydenham called on teachers to use the events of the war to teach children moral lessons connected with the history and ideals of the nation, which would serve as a monument to those who had sacrificed their lives for their country. Many must have felt that the current debate raging over the need for conscription proved that not enough was being done in schools to teach young people the duties and responsibilities of citizenship. What was the point of teaching children that they were part of a great people who had created a great empire, if they left school unwilling to fight to defend that empire?

Admiral the Lord Beresford, in a Foreword to H.W. Household's history of the navy for children, echoed this sentiment, explaining that teachers had an important role to play in 'making the character of our future citizens' and that:

> There can be no finer training for a child than the inculcation of a lofty and ennobling spirit of patriotism, and in no way can the patriotism of the British child be so successfully aroused as by the stirring story of our splendid fighting seamen.[32]

The benefit of using the stories of great soldiers and sailors of the past was that they could be adapted to appeal to children of all ages. Unlike much of the history and geography teaching, which was aimed at older children, perhaps ten and over, exciting tales of adventure and battle could be told to younger children, thus inspiring them to greatness at an early age. Indeed, many children would already be familiar with the language of such tales from their fictional literature, discussed in Chapter 3, so it was no wonder that patriots recognised the opportunity of adapting the lives of military leaders into exciting tales for younger children.

Even at the age of seven, Minnie Cowley, who grew up in Whitton, near Richmond in London, during the war, says that the ideals of patriotism, king and empire were 'crammed' into them at school. She remembers that celebrations such as Empire Day, begun in 1906 and celebrated on 24 May, were always a big occasion, with the children excited to dress up as Britannia and wave their Union Jacks during the singing of the National Anthem.[33] But the war allowed the teachers at Cowley's infant school further opportunities to instil pride and patriotism in the children:

> Lots of soldiers marched past our school almost every day, and the crunching sound of their heavy boots on the stony ground was so noisy that we could not hear the teacher. Taking us out to the playground to see them as they went by in a long line, she told us that they were all brave men who were going to stop the Germans making us slaves.[34]

Cowley's father was a master plasterer, who enlisted as soon as war was declared:

> I was only a little girl of seven, but I almost burst with pride: my Dad looked just like a king ready to lead his armies into battle.[35]

At school the teachers would line the children up in the playground and, calling on them to march like soldiers, lead them in singing:

> My Daddy's dressed in khaki,
> He's gone away to fight
> For King and Home and Country
> For Honour and for Right.
> We do not want the Germans
> To get all over here
> So Dad must go and fight them,
> We'll never, never fear.
> Now give three cheers for Daddy,
> We would not keep him back,

> For we are little Britons
> And love the Union Jack.[36]

Cowley says:

> How I loved that part of the day! I would march along, all stiff and
> straight, singing louder than any of the others and imagining I was
> my Dad. Of course, there were some children whose fathers were
> not soldiers, and I would tell them they should not sing with us,
> because their dads were not fighting the Germans, but were cowardy
> custards.[37]

Several books for children devoted to the responsibilities of citizenship also appeared during the war. One, entitled *Children of the Empire*,
explained the position to children like this:

> You are a member of a family, and that family is part of a nation. All
> the people who live in our land are united by their history, language,
> religion, customs and institutions. For this reason, they come to love
> their country, and loving it, they wish to work for it, to defend its
> liberties and to protect its honour.

> This love and service of your country is patriotism. Patriotism is a
> sense of our responsibility for our country; each citizen of a country
> has to take his share in the work. Every child should be a patriot.[38]

The book goes on to explain the development and structure of the
English parliamentary and legal systems as well as the forms of gov-
ernance throughout the empire, ending with a chapter outlining the
citizens' 'Duty to Empire'. Here children are advised to think what they
might do for the empire in their future lives, and urged to think of their
future career not only in terms of what it will give to them, but also of
how it will help benefit the Empire. It explains:

> At no time in the recent history of Britain will there have been such a
> chance for both boys and girls as there will be after the war. It will be
> left to those now growing up to remake Britain ... None must suppose
> that patriotism is needed only in time of war, and by soldiers. The
> greatness of a country depends on the greatness of spirit with which
> every kind of duty is undertaken by its citizens. The home-maker is
> as essential as the defender of homes.[39]

Conscription had proved to many imperialists and conservatives that the duties of citizenship were not fully appreciated by the British people. Not all men had understood that it was their responsibility to fight to defend their country; they had had to be compelled to do it. If this was to be avoided in the future, and if Britain was to sustain her position as a leading military and industrial power, then her future leaders and workers had to be taught to understand the nature of citizenship. It was not enough to leave it to the few; if Britain was to rebuild then children must understand that there was serious work to be done. This book and others emphasised the need for everyone to take their places as citizens of the empire.

Although we cannot know exactly which books and what methods of teaching were being used in which schools, we can gather from Board of Education and School Inspectors' reports that the war was a regular subject for study, particularly in the higher grades in elementary schools and in secondary schools. Despite the undoubted interest of both pupils and teachers in the war, School Inspectors occasionally questioned the quality of war-themed classes. One, inspecting a school in a northern district in 1914, remarked in his report to the Board of Education that he felt the teaching about the war was being overdone:

> In the Upper Departments, perhaps history teaching suffered most. The teachers rushed into schemes following the course of the war; and their lessons were mere reproductions of newspaper headings which the children knew before they came to school.[40]

Another, inspecting schools in the south-east, wrote that he considered too much time had been sacrificed to 'a nebulous War History' and over-ambitious schemes of teaching. He recommended instead that teachers take a broader outline, charting the history of the combatant nations through the eighteenth and nineteenth centuries, making regular reference to the present war.[41]

Perhaps the surprise development came in English lessons, where inspectors commented on the great improvement they saw in children's English composition, which they attributed to the interest the children had in their subject. They saw an improvement in general knowledge as children wrote compositions on war topics, including the War Loan and the War Taxes, but they were struck most by children's letter writing. 'Letter writing is now a real thing: composition is improved by virtue of the greater wealth of experience to write about', wrote one inspector of schools in the north. Another felt that:

> Real letters to real persons are being written. In a town school the
> letters to the men at the front were so interesting that I enquired
> and found that 95 per cent of the children had relatives in the
> service.[42]

We have already considered how letter writing helped families to sustain their relationships during the war, but it seems clear from the school inspectors' reports that this correspondence was also having a positive effect on children's education. Reading such letters, it becomes clear that, while their class teacher may have envisaged these as simple composition exercises, they were much more than that to the children. Perhaps for the first time, these children were using their lessons in composition to construct genuine letters to people they loved. Into them they could pour all their news about home and school, and in return expect a personal letter that might tell them something of their father or brother's experience in the war they were so interested to learn about. Perhaps it was not that the children had a 'greater wealth of experience to write about' but simply that for the first time they had someone they wanted to write to. Unlike previous exercises in composition, which may have seemed contrived and mechanical, these letters were an expression of the children's need to communicate with their absent relatives. As such, these were hardly lessons at all, but personal attempts to bridge the gulf the war had created between them and their fathers, their brothers, and even unknown soldiers.

So perhaps it was part patriotic duty and part intelligent teaching that prompted schools to encourage their pupils to include letters in the parcels of cigarettes and clothing they collected and sent out to the troops from school.

Encouraged by teachers and parents, children sent messages of support to soldiers they had never met, and in return received letters of thanks.

The collection at the Imperial War Museum shows that some children and soldiers exchanged a single letter, while others began a correspondence that lasted the duration of the war and beyond.

The pupils at St John's School on the Isle of Dogs in East London were one such group of children, who were each given the name of a particular soldier and encouraged to knit and send parcels to them. Amy Griffiths, eight years old in 1914, sent a letter to Sergeant J. Hancock of the 1st Battalion Royal Fusiliers accompanying her parcel in the first months of the war. Although Amy's letter to Sergeant Hancock does not survive, we can imagine its tone and content from the reply she received. Sergeant Hancock wrote to Amy on 11 October 1914, saying:

> I am writing to thank you for your kindness in sending me the tobacco cigarettes, it was very kind of you, I'm afraid you've given me rather a hard task in telling me to kill all the Germ-Huns, but I'll do my best for you. I'm afraid I can't manage the Kaiser as he won't come anywhere near me unfortunately, but I'll give him a look-up when we get to Berlin. The Germans serenade us in the evenings with their national songs, and we give them a cheer when they finish, and invite them over to our trenches, but they are too shy.
>
> Please thank your friends for their kindness and accept my thanks for yourself. I hope this will find you in the best of health.
>
> Goodbye, yours faithfully, J. Hancock[43]

This letter displays the cheery optimism of the early days of the war, when the volunteer army believed the fight would be short and victorious. That the eight-year-old Amy was already versed in the language of war propaganda, referring to the Germ-Huns, is no surprise when you consider the mood of anti-German sentiment that swept the nation in the lead up to, and first months of, the war.[44] But Sergeant Hancock's subsequent letters to Amy, which, after the first one, were sent to her home address, begin to hint at the difference in the soldiers' and civilians' developing perceptions of their enemy. In January 1915 Hancock writes to Amy telling her of the Christmas truce which occurred at places on the Western Front. The letter, very different in tone from the last, suggests a newfound respect for the men on the other side of no-man's-land.

> I spent a rather interesting if not a happy Xmas, we made a truce with the enemy opposite us they are only 60 yrds away and exchanged cigarettes, papers etc, a lot of them could speak English, they are Saxons and object to being called Germans they said they would be very glad when the war was finished, but they firmly believe they are going to win, I have enclosed one of their postcards with the chaps name on who gave it to me. We are having very rainy weather and our trenches are like little rivers, and are not at all pleasant to live in. Please excuse this awful scribble, as writing is rather a difficult job.

Other children sent gifts and letters to groups of soldiers they did not know as part of a whole school effort, but many still received an individual reply. In December 1915, seven-year-old Bertha Wadey received a letter from a Lieutenant H.N. Hignett, serving in the 1/5th Battalion Cheshire Regiment in France, thanking her for the parcel of gifts she had sent out to the Battalion from Dulwich Hamlet School. The officer does not seem to be conscious of any need to hide the conditions of trench warfare from the seven-year-old, or resent the extra work of having to write and thank her:

> I have only time to write you a very short letter, but I wish to thank you very much for the tin of Vaseline which I kept for myself out of the big box of things which came from your school. You don't know how glad I was to have it last night. The trenches were half full of water and freezing at the time. As there was a biting cold wind I smeared my face and hands with Vaseline and so kept them from getting chapped with the frost. It is most awfully kind of you all to send these things out to the men who were all very pleased with them.
>
> Wishing you a very happy Xmas and New Year,
>
> Yours sincerely,
>
> H.N. Hignett

This letter is accompanied in the archive by a certificate of gratitude to Bertha from the Overseas Club, a patriotic organisation established 'to promote the unity of British Subjects the world over'. Groups like the Overseas Club and the Girls Patriotic Union were active in organising and recognising the work children did for the war effort. They awarded certificates and ribbons in recognition of children's contribution, and the large numbers of them deposited in the Imperial War Museum suggests that the recipients treasured them as tokens of their part in the 'official' war effort.

Other schools focused their attention on wounded soldiers convalescing in their local area. Many collected food, newspapers and magazines and even paid personal visits to cheer the men, often recuperating far from home. For these men, often horribly scarred both physically and mentally, we cannot be sure how welcome these visits were. But without close family nearby, and perhaps because of their naïve interest, wounded soldiers occasionally wrote to the children of the horrors they had experienced and the frustration they now felt. Alice Waterhouse, a school girl at Parochial School, Aughton, received such a letter after collecting food for the patients at a military hospital in Moss Side, Liverpool. Lance Corporal H. Bearer wrote to Alice in June 1915:

> Just a few lines hoping you are in the very best of health. I am pleased to let you know that I am feeling a little better considering I have been in hospital over 8 months now. Also I wish to thank you very much for your kindness in giving me those eggs which I heartily enjoyed for my tea.
>
> I was buried alive by a shell bursting in front of my trench while I was on observation post for nearly three days before being dug out.
>
> This is the ninth hospital I have been in. I was in six different hospitals in Manchester before being sent to Maghull so I must thank God I am alive. You may remember me I passed by your school in the wheelchair about two weeks ago. I would like to write you a few lines to thank you for your kindness to me. God bless you with success and good health these are my sincere wishes to you. My kind regards and best respects to you and your teacher.
>
> Sincerely yours
>
> 7338 L/Cpl H Bearer

For some children and soldiers, these donations and visits to hospital started up relationships that lasted throughout the war and beyond. Ten-year-old Doris Tickner struck up one such friendship with Private Mick Teulan, an Australian soldier serving with the 5th Division AIF. Private Teulan had been injured by a shell in France and was recovering at Spalding Hall Convalescent Home in Golders Green, North London, near to where the Tickner family lived. The Imperial War Museum archive contains 55 letters written to Doris between 1917 and 1919, mainly by Mick but also by both his sisters and his wife in Australia. The relationship was clearly of great importance to the whole Teulan family, separated by thousands of miles as well as the war itself.[45] Teulan's wife and sisters thank the whole Tickner family for their support and refer to packages and presents they have sent from Australia. Mick often asks why he has not heard from Doris for some time as he is moved around the country and then eventually back to France, but she is clearly a fairly regular correspondent.

When he is eventually sent back to France in the spring of 1918, Teulan jokes to Doris that he is unlikely to see her again until he gets another wound and is sent back to England:

> You see I have taken your advice this time I am letting all the shells go by and just at present there are any amount of them flying about our own and German ones. They are going over the ground where we are camped and I am not in the deep dug out either in fact there are only a few pieces of wood covering me, not enough to stop a shell if it happens to fall on it. I will try to arrange to get to a hospital where you can visit if I am lucky enough to get back to England again.

In September 1918 Teulan was in England again after being shot through the wrist, and joked to Doris: 'certainly I thought that it was only the shells that I was to dodge. You did not mention bullets, bombs or grenade, nor Gas'. Mick Teulan survived the war and returned to Australia in 1919.

The fact that the process of correspondence often outlived the initial exchange of gifts and thanks, developing into fledgling friendships, shows how much importance was attached to the link by both the children themselves and the soldiers to whom they wrote. Here we see men writing genuine, kind, uncondescending letters of thanks and goodwill to small children they had never met. They appear truly touched by the interest of the children, and, particularly for those men with no family close by, the relationships they formed through the letters probably helped sustain them throughout the war. For the schools, encouraging the children to write to men they had never met was a way of highlighting to them the enormity of the war effort. By adopting a soldier at the Front or in hospital children were ensured a personal connection to the war regardless of whether they had a relative involved in the fighting.

Increasingly, as the war continued, the duties of citizenship and the role of children in rebuilding the country after the war entered the curriculum with the teaching of geography and history. The Board of Education and individual teachers aimed to maintain a rigorous standard of intellectual accuracy and to avoid the tendency to subvert lessons in history and geography to serve the British position. Some children had responded by throwing themselves into their work, as they found their lessons more relevant than ever before, and this produced improvements in the standard and diversity of their work. The underlying message to children was that the British position was not only the right one, but, in fact, the only one a nation with such a history of greatness could take. Children learnt their place within a noble Empire and in the context of a history filled with great deeds and great sacrifices. It was fervently hoped that these children would learn their lessons and be fit to maintain these traditions when the war was over and they took their places as full citizens of the British Empire.

London schools go to war

> There is no doubt that the resumption of the normal work of the schools at this crisis, and the silent influence exercised by the teachers through children and parents upon homes in every part of London, materially contributed to preserving the mental and moral balance of the capital of the Empire at this juncture, and the Council has placed on record its sense of the value of the teachers' services.[46]
>
> London County Council – Annual Report
> for Education 1915–1919

London's schools were closed for the summer holidays when war broke out in August 1914, but fears about the uncertainty of what effect the war might have on the capital prompted the London County Council (LCC) to ask all their teachers to return to London and reopen the schools. The idea that schoolteachers would have a 'silent influence' on the moral and mental balance of children and families across the capital was part of the Council's vision for an education service that encompassed more than just the teaching of facts to young children. Education, in the eyes of the LCC, was a force for good in society and, if run effectively, held the promise of positive change. The LCC had a history of embracing new educational theories and methods and aimed to train its teachers to the highest standards. Thus, the children educated under this enlightened system would be raised up from their humble beginnings by the acquisition of knowledge, and the ennobling efforts of their teachers. Before the war the Council's philosophy was to best educate London's children to be useful citizens of the capital of the British Empire. That philosophy acquired a new sense of urgency during the war as the Council recognised the essential role of education in moulding a new generation, capable and keen to rebuild a better Britain.

At the outbreak of war there was optimism in London about the future of education. Members of the Education Department, led by its Education Officer Robert Blair, supported calls for the raising of the school leaving age, and for the increase of secondary provision through both technical schools and the scholarship scheme. Attention was also being paid to teaching methods and the curriculum through the influence of educational psychologists and reformers speaking regularly in the capital.[47]

As elsewhere in the country, the first consequence of the war for London schools was the shortage of teaching staff, only partially solved by the secondment of female teachers from girls' and infant departments and by the return of married or retired teachers to the classroom.[48] Blair considered, however, that London's children still learnt important lessons despite the disruption and teacher shortages:

> The deepest lessons that were learnt in the schools during the war cannot be gauged by external evidence. The appeal of heroism, the touch of sympathy, may seem to have but a transient influence on the heart of youth, but they have probably sunk deeper than would appear and may bear abundant fruit in after life.[49]

It was felt that the war gave teachers an opportunity to break through the normal routine of school lessons and challenged everybody to re-examine old thoughts and assumptions. Shortages of staff, materials and books were overcome as imaginatively as possible; instead of visiting museums and galleries – most of which had closed – teachers took children to performances of Shakespeare at the Old Vic. It was accepted that losing teachers must be detrimental, but it was believed that other things partly counter-balanced the loss

> by the stimulus of stirring scenes, by the story of thrilling deeds, by the desire for personal service, and by the ready response made by the children to the call to 'do their bit' for their country both at school and at home.[50]

The records of individual schools in the capital show that children were indeed ready to 'do their bit'. At Cobourg Road Girls' School the children supported the 68th Battery R. F. A., sending parcels and letters to the soldiers every month. The children were 'rapturous' on the arrival of replies from the soldiers, and some men, including the commanding officer, visited the school while home on leave. In recognition of the children's support, the men of the 68th Battery later honoured the girls with a commemorative shield and the school produced its own war record documenting the efforts of the children.[51]

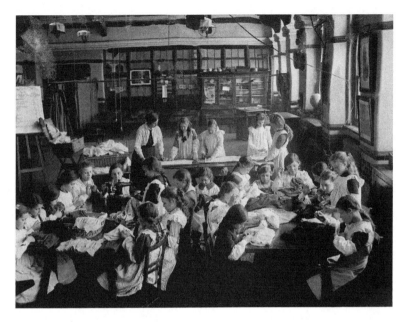

Figure 5.2   Children from Gibbons Road School in Willesden, London, make articles of clothing
Source: Imperial War Museum.

Other activities popular in schools included making clothing or splints and crutches with materials and instruction supplied by local depots. The children's efforts were always praised by the schools, which were keen to take advantage of the children's willingness to sacrifice their free time and pocket money, to press home to them a message of self-denial and hard work. In a letter to the December 1915 issue of the school magazine, the Headmaster of Wood Close LCC School wrote:

> You, boys, have done, and are doing, your share, and you ought to rejoice in the feeling that you have done your duty. *'Duty'* and *'sacrifice'* are two of the best words in the English language, and the more we can carry out their true meaning, the more shall we be really satisfied with ourselves. Keep on trying and you will be really surprised at the feeling of happiness gradually springing up within you in spite of the difficulties thereof.[52]

The war was a perfect opportunity for schools to use as an example to their pupils of the higher ideals of discipline and sacrifice. Children could be encouraged to think of themselves as future useful citizens, to work hard and behave so that they might one day prove good workers. This was not a new message; before the war children had been told of the threats to the stability of the British Empire as an attempt to encourage them to see themselves as its future defenders. Now the real threat of defeat could be held up as an example of what could happen if a country and its people failed to do their duty.

Schools were hugely proud of their old boys, and the exploits and memory of these former pupils were invoked as an example to the younger boys. At Brecknock School in Tufnell Park, North London, the school occasionally closed for half a day to honour old boys who had been awarded military honours, and the headmaster recorded all the letters he received from old boys in uniform in the school's log book.[53] Schools were also often visited by old boys home on leave. Robert Blair makes a special mention of this tie between schools and their old boys in his report on London's schools during the war. He even cites one example of a school that started a fund to provide for the education of one old boy's children after he had been killed in France.[54]

Despite this commitment to supporting the war effort, Blair believed educational standards in London's schools did not suffer. In this he was not alone; the LCC's Chief Examiner for Junior County Scholarships examined the work of some 10,000 children who competed for scholarships in the last year of the war, and actually felt standards were improving. The examiner had expected the number of students getting high marks to fall, but in fact the numbers rose. They rose so much that he dismissed any possibility of its being the result of a change of standard in questions or marking, and concluded that children and teachers were working harder despite the obvious difficulties they had to overcome.[55]

Children in London were also encouraged to contribute to the war effort through the War Savings campaign. In London arrangements were made between the War Savings Committee and the Council for teachers to organise the distribution of War Savings Certificates to the children in their schools. Almost all the schools took part, and in over 100 elementary schools children collected over £2000. Although the LCC was unsure of exact figures, it estimated that the elementary and secondary schools of London raised over £500,000.[56]

As well as issues of staffing and curriculum, the war also affected the practicalities of schooling London's children. In total, 13 of the capital's schools were completely taken over by the War Office, meaning that their children had to be accommodated by neighbouring schools.

Figure 5.3 Pupils from Gibbons Road School in Willesden, London, line up to receive certificates for contributing 15 shillings and 6 pence to their War Saving Association in 1916. The board to the left shows the different war charities which have benefited from the school's pupils and staff, including the Dollis Hill Military Hospital and the British and Foreign Sailors Society
Source: Imperial War Museum.

In some instances overcrowding meant that children only attended school on a half-time basis. The most serious threat to the day-to-day management of the schools, however, came from air raids. Relatively little disruption or damage was done to school buildings by the night-time visits of German Zeppelins. It was the daytime aeroplane raids that caused problems. This problem was one that schools and the Council were forced to deal with throughout the war, but the most terrible incident occurred on the morning of 13 June 1917, when a bomb fell on the North Street School in Poplar, killing 18 children and injuring many others. Blair wrote:

> From that time forward it was realised that London had come within the fighting zone, and that those who were responsible for the children's education were also responsible for doing their utmost to safeguard the children's lives.[57]

The most difficult decision facing the Council was whether to advise schools to send their children home at the first sound of an air raid or whether to keep them at school. In July 1917, the Department wrote to the head teachers of London schools. Blair accepted that neither choice was completely free from risk, but wrote that the schools were generally a safer place for the children to be. There were roughly 1,000 school buildings in the capital and the Council felt that the risk of one being hit was fairly low. Any risk had to be weighed against the alternative of sending London's 650,000 children out into the streets, where they would be at just as much risk, if not more, from bombs and shrapnel.

The Council was aware how frightening air raids could be for children, and wrote:

> While it is recognised that it may not be possible to carry on work of a normal character during an actual raid, it is most desirable that the attention of the children, particularly young children, should as far as possible be drawn from the raid itself. This has been accomplished successfully in many cases by letting the children sing or by telling them stories.[58]

The need to keep the children calm was important both in terms of safety and for morale. Here was another way that teachers could exercise their 'silent influence' over the children, both to show them how to behave and to allay their fears. The Council urged schools to be a force for morale in the community, saying that the schools had already done much to

> allay the anxiety of parents and particularly to induce them to leave their children in the school buildings entirely under the control of the teachers until all danger has passed. It is felt that the confidence of the parents in the teachers is so great that any danger of panic due to excitement may by such appeals be reduced to the smallest proportions.[59]

Parents' confidence in the teachers and their faith in the safety of leaving their children in school were not complete, however, and school keepers were instructed to lock all outside gates and refuse admission to all unauthorised persons as soon as a raid was sounded. Schools were also told that they would have the support of the police should parents crowding at the school gates become a problem. The catastrophe in Poplar had shaken parents and the schools alike, and shortly afterwards the Council suggested the school send out the following letter to the parents of children in their care:

My Dear Mothers,

The County Council has again decided that, in spite of the sad trouble in —, the children are, on the whole, safest in school, and that we MUST keep them until the danger is past, whatever the time may be.

May I beg of you, for your sakes, your children's sakes, and for our sakes NOT to come up for them?

1. Even if the schools had warning and we all let them out, three quarters of a million children all over London would be toddling home in the streets, many a long way, lots of them with no mothers with them and some of them with no mothers at home when they got there.

Ten times more children would be killed and hurt, and many would see awful sights which might haunt them for life.

2. If the mothers were also crowding round the schools and in the streets, they would also be injured, and mothers' lives are very, very precious to their children, to their homes and to our country.

3. If some mothers came up and not others, we should never have time to pick out the right children, all the others would cry, and there would still be the double danger to mothers and children in the streets.

4. Even if you do come up, we CANNOT let them out, so keep indoors for the children's sakes.

5. Our school has a concrete roof. A bomb could scarcely come through to us, but a bomb on the roof would hurt lots of you outside, so please don't come near us.

6. Your children are nearly as precious to us as to you. We have ... to care for and we will take every care of them and keep them happy. They won't even know what is going on if we can help it. Isn't that much better?

I am, etc.[60]

This letter addressing itself solely to mothers articulates many of the preoccupations the authorities had with regard to families during the war.

It recognises that an increasing number of married women had taken up employment to supplement their separation allowance, or simply to take advantage of the relatively high wages on offer in the factories, resulting in a perceived breakdown of authority in the home. Officials were worried that with men away fighting and women out at work children were more likely to become delinquent. The letter also reflects the increasing importance placed on the status of motherhood during wartime, when huge losses on the battlefield produced an emphasis on the importance of bearing and raising the future generation.[61] Just as it had during the 'national efficiency' debates of the pre-war years, motherhood became a national concern, prompting calls for increased efforts to reduce maternal mortality and promote better services for mothers and infants.[62]

Some improvements in family health *were* seen during the war. Because of the increased wages earned by parents, and the separation allowance received by mothers, children in the less prosperous districts of London were better fed and clothed than they had been before the war. The number of children deemed to be 'necessitous' by the Council fell from 75,000 in the early days of the war to just over 8,000 at its close. School medical inspections showed that the number of children found to be poorly nourished during 1918 was less than half the number in 1913.[63] But the medical inspections also drew attention to some new medical problems for London's children:

> During 1916 and 1917 some increase in nervous manifestations among children was observed as a sequel to air-raids, but this condition was purely temporary and no permanent ill effect has been observed.[64]

Since this was only written in 1919, it seems early to be contending that 'no permanent ill effect' had occurred. In fact, the psychological effect of the air raids was very unpredictable; some children were thrilled by the drama and novelty of the experience, while others were terrified of the sound and even more horrified when the planes or Zeppelins were brought down, knowing that men had been killed.

Just seven years old when war broke out, Minnie Cowley experienced a real conflict of emotions whenever an air raid warning sounded near to her home in Whitton.

> I was scared and excited at the same time. Scared in case the German aeroplanes came down in our road and lots of soldiers got out and

killed us all, excited because there were so many people in our house.[65]

The Germans had begun air raids over the UK in December 1914, using both aeroplanes and Zeppelins. By June 1918, 108 raids had been flown over Great Britain, with the south-east the most heavily targeted area. By the end of the war civilian casualties reached 5,611, with 1,413 people being killed by air attacks.[66] More significant, perhaps, than the attacks themselves was the fear they provoked amongst the general population. The relatively new and exciting world of aviation was transformed into a terrifying and violent menace. For the first time civilians came under attack in their own homes. Susan Grayzel asserts that these attacks on the oft-cited 'innocent women and children' of London transformed the relationship between combatants and civilians and between the state and home. Air raids helped cement the notion of 'total' war, as all could now be victims of German aggression, and all could display the virtues of stoicism and bravery which could contribute to victory. At the same time, the state, including the Board of Education and the LCC, was forced to confront the need to protect its citizens at home.[67]

Kathleen Betterton, whose father was a liftman on the London Underground and had been declared medically unfit for active service, lived in Fulham as a child. She remembers how excited she and the daughter of a family they sheltered with were at the prospect of a raid:

> Those nights held for the two of us all the fun of midnight picnics, and my hopeful question, as I was tucked up in bed, was always – 'do you think there'll be an air-raid?' In the morning on our way to school we hunted for bits of shrapnel to pass from hand to hand round the class, and we would swap our stories of the night's doings like any grown-up.[68]

Arthur Jacobs was born in 1907 and lived in Hampstead as a child. He remembers being woken in the night by his parents in order to watch the first Zeppelin being brought down. As the Zeppelin fell to the earth he heard a cheer go up amongst his neighbours, but remembers that their landlady shouted:

> 'For God's sake don't <u>cheer</u>, there are poor devils dying up there!'[69]

It was a dramatic event, and Jacobs recalls being confused about his feelings on the night:

I couldn't take in the tragedy of it, feeling the situation to be no more real than if I had been at the cinema. If I had any feeling at all it was one of selfish relief – for now there wouldn't be a horrible bang which shook the crockery on the kitchen dresser and made me jump nearly out of my skin.[70]

Dr C.W. Kimmins, Chief Inspector of Schools for the LCC, was particularly interested in the children's response to the air raids. In 1915 he set 945 children between the ages of 8 and 13, spread across five different schools, the task of writing essays on their impressions of the London air raids. In a lecture to the Child Study Society at the Royal Sanitary Institute, Dr Kimmins analysed the results, explaining that:

At eight years of age, the noise of the firing bulked very largely in the essays. No personal feelings were expressed and there was no evidence of fear. Even at that age the girls looked after the younger children. At nine the boys thoroughly enjoyed the raid, spending as much time as possible in the streets; occasionally among the girls great fear was expressed. At ten the boy was very talkative, and for the first time there was distinct evidence of fear, though not nearly so marked as in the case of the girls.[71]

Kimmins noted that throughout there was evidence of the mothering attitude of girls towards the more helpless and that boys appeared to get more confident, becoming obsessed with finding souvenirs of the raids at around 12. One striking point noted by Kimmins was the evidence of the very small part played by the father in the family. He noted that in 95 per cent of the essays no references at all were made to fathers (in some cases, no doubt, because the fathers were away fighting), but that even when they were mentioned the references were far from flattering, with men described as terrified and abandoning their families to seek solace in the pub.

Kimmins believed that the essays illustrated the dangers of suppressed emotions amongst the children, with girls of 12 the most at risk, as they clearly felt frightened but would not show it. What is interesting is that, although he is aware of the dangers of suppressed emotion, Kimmins appears to take the children's essays at face value. Nowhere does he suggest the possibility that some of the children may have been concealing their fears on paper. While Kimmins' interpretation of these essays (which unfortunately have not survived) is a fascinating insight into a contemporary attempt to understand children's attitudes, we mustn't forget that these children, surrounded by their peers and writing for a complete stranger, might not always have admitted what they really felt.

On another occasion, at the West Ham and District Educational Conference, Dr Kimmins delivered an address on 'The Attitude of London Children Towards the War'. Based on further essays, and his conversations with children across London, Kimmins noted that the girls were 'more mature and thoughtful than the boys: but the general tone throughout was intensely loyal, calm and courageous'. He went on to outline the practical things the children had been doing for the war effort, then explained:

> As regards thrift, the girls frequently mentioned instances of their own activity in this direction; the boys were fond of giving good advice, including such items as 'save a penny a week and win the war!' but, so far as the essays showed, they were content with merely advising. Both sexes were strong on cutting down expenditure on sweets and cinemas; the boys also mentioned going without comics and similar literature; the girls never. Minor economies included fireworks (boys), light (girls), and on the part of one 'typical boy', soap![72]

Kimmins was also interested in the children's domestic life and how they coped with the war at home, noting:

> The girls obviously took much more kindly to practical helpfulness in the home than the boys, particularly in the matter of 'minding baby'. Many of the boys seemed to regard as their main duty at home, refraining from worrying, and, as one put it, keeping 'merry and bright'.[73]

Dr Kimmins concluded that, in terms of children's general attitude to the war, little girls of ten and boys of 11 were the most bellicose and bloodthirsty. Older girls of 13 or so were by far the most thoughtful, 'and got down to principles as the basis of the statements they made'.[74]

What is interesting here is how the children's writing appears to match the intentions of the schools with regard to the war. The children's attitudes are described as being 'intensely loyal, calm and courageous', very much in keeping with the intentions of their teachers.

In taking responsibility for the children during air raids, the Education Department was hoping to set an example to parents of 'business as usual'. They wanted to prevent panic and disruption and as far as possible carry on the normal practice of schooling. The war upset much of the department's work, from the building and repair of its school buildings to the training of its future staff. But it also focused public interest on the subject of education, and on the health and welfare of children, as people looked to create a better future after the war. Blair pointed to the forthcoming 1918 Education Act as the culmination of this increased interest and recognition of the importance of education during the war. He observed that the vital relation of education to national destiny was indicated by the fact that the Bill was being discussed by Parliament at the very moment of the great German offensive of 1918, and that it received its Royal Assent just as Haig was beginning his triumphant attack on 8 August 1918. Blair concluded his report on the war years by saying:

> It may be taken as a good omen that the new campaign against ignorance should have been launched upon the day that inaugurated the crowning attack upon tyranny. For complete freedom cannot be established until ignorance has been dethroned, and the foundations of peace will not be finally secure until they are based upon widespread knowledge. The training of enlightened citizens is the greatest problem for the next few decades, and national education is the master key to national reconstruction.[75]

Conclusion

Throughout the war teachers and children responded enthusiastically to the challenges of war. Both sought to incorporate it into the curriculum, perhaps a recognition on the part of teachers that in this new age of child-centred learning they would be failing their pupils if they ignored a subject so closely linked to so many families. The war inspired new lessons in history and geography, but it was perhaps as a vehicle for lessons on citizenship that the war proved to be most useful. By extolling the virtues of past and present military heroes, as well as the ordinary soldiers who served under them, schools attempted to instil in their pupils the importance of duty and sacrifice. Children learnt about the extent of the British Empire, its role and its responsibilities, and highlighting the threat to its security encouraged children to want to work and fight for its survival in the future.

Across the country individual schools worked hard to overcome the difficulties of teacher shortages and absent pupils to maintain a high standard of education throughout the war. They found ways for their pupils to take an active role in the home front war effort, both as a means of materially contributing to the successful prosecution of the war, and also as a way of further bringing home to the children the duties of citizenship. Children collected, made and saved anything and everything for the war effort, while maintaining bonds and striking up new friendships with soldiers serving abroad.

In many ways the war seems to have energised teachers, children and schools. It appears that, in working hard to overcome the difficulties imposed by war, they not only overcame them, but in many instances superseded them. Teachers and educationalists at all levels from the Board of Education down to individual classrooms never lost their pre-war enthusiasm for educational reform. Instead, they continued to press for change throughout the war, highlighting the importance of their work, educating the citizens of the future to take up the work of reconstruction and reform after the war was over.

Education continued to be debated throughout the war, and the new Education Act finally became law in 1918. The Act gave the Board of Education powers to compel local authorities to develop their educational provision, while in turn it committed the state to providing aid in proportion to local expenditure. This provided for the establishment of nursery schools, continuation schools and more post-elementary provision, through both secondary schools and the 'trade' schools. The half-time system was completely abolished and 14 became the uniform compulsory school leaving age.

Passed on a wave of optimism, many of the provisions of the Act were to be short-lived. The economic depression of 1921 forced the government to form a committee, under Sir Eric Geddes, to consider cuts in public spending. The 'Geddes Axe' reduced funds for education by a third.[76] The major sacrifices were the abandonment of the idea of continuation schools and a curtailment of the increased spending on nursery provision, reflecting the need to concentrate resources on the core elementary and secondary-aged pupils. Despite this, much of the thinking behind the 1918 Act went on to inform the education debate up until the Second World War.

6
Conclusion

The way in which British children were mobilised for war in 1914–1918 is symbolic of the nature of total war. The mobilisation of the Home Front was intended to complement the battle front, as each side was urged to work harder for the sake of the other. As Tammy Proctor has argued, the civilian/soldier dichotomy helped to sell the idea of war.[1] The fact that the war touched children's lives at home, at school, in their youth groups and in their private games illustrates the enormity of the war's influence over life in Britain at that time. Little attempt was made to shield children from the war because their support was vital for Britain's present and future. Adult society believed children could contribute materially and psychologically to the successful prosecution of the war, and children themselves were keen to become involved because of the impact it was having on their family lives. The war was a national endeavour, requiring the participation of all. Most significantly, children's mobilisation was considered to be a lesson in citizenship, teaching them the importance of service to the nation, something essential for the future regeneration of Britain.

During the war itself, most children's connection to the war was personal. Millions of children had a relative in the army, and those who did not had friends, neighbours and teachers connected to the war. For children with a father or brother away from home, the most significant impact of the war was this domestic upheaval. Not all will have been sorry to see fathers go; A.L. Rowse considers that his father's absence was 'a great blessing'; but many others were deeply troubled.[2] As the war continued these children grew up. Fathers missed years of the day-to-day lives of their children, and the only way for both parties to compensate for this was through the exchange of letters.

155

For many children letters were a hugely significant element of their war experience. Letters became the emotional channel through which families supported each other for months at a time and over several years. They represented the ties of love and support which sustained the relationship between the Home Front and fighting line.[3] In their letters children told their fathers about their lives at home and in return their fathers told them something of the war they were experiencing. But men did this carefully, and the way in which they described their war to their children offers us evidence of their attempts at emotional survival. In their letters fathers became semi-fictional characters creating a narrative in which they could appear quite safe. In order to maintain their bonds with their children, fathers needed their children to be able to picture them. At first they achieved this by concentrating on domestic scenes, describing their living conditions, their food and the people and animals they met from day to day. But as the war went on this was not enough. They had been gone too long for these illusions of shared experience to be enough. They wanted their children to understand where they were and what they were doing. To reconcile themselves and their children to their new role, these soldier–fathers often reverted to the language of fantasy and play that had sustained their own pre-war understanding of combat. They presented the war as fun and exciting, comparing it to childhood games in order both to please their children and, perhaps, to allay their own fears.

When these men returned, it was to families that had survived without them for several years. Relationships needed to be rebuilt, roles defined and feelings reaffirmed. Men had longed for their families while they were away, and children had pined for their fathers, but on return the reality didn't always match the ideal. Many autobiographers mention the strain of living with their fathers in the years following the war. Some men found it hard to readjust, and it was often families who bore the brunt of that process. When domestic violence flared it was blamed on the brutalising effects of warfare, and contemporaries could easily believe that aggression and violence had become men's ingrained response.[4] It was felt that a return to normalcy was needed, and that this could best be achieved through the redefinition of gender roles and by women's return to the domestic sphere.[5] Scholars of the interwar period have noted the renewed energy with which people focused on the domestic, on the home, the family and marriage. Private relationships came to be seen as an indicator of national health, and the mending and strengthening of the relationship between the sexes was vital to the rebuilding of British society after the war.[6]

Generational divides also needed to be re-established. Children, during the war, had been encouraged to imagine themselves as adults. Provided with props by toy manufacturers and parents, children could create miniature versions of the war with toy soldiers, guns, planes and battleships. Alternatively, they could dress themselves as soldiers and shoot each other with imitation guns. Evidence suggests that, even when children had no toys available, they were still keen to play war games. They could make their own toy guns with what they found lying around and could fight over territory as they had before the war, changing their imaginary battlefield from the Imperial Colonies to the Western Front. This can be seen as further evidence for Audoin-Rouzeau and Becker's theory of 'war culture', whereby children's toys, games and ephemera become part of that 'collection of representations of the conflict which crystallised into a system of thought which gave the war its deep significance'.[7]

After the war, once popular support had turned to public revulsion at the ceaseless violence of war, adult society was less keen to encourage children to emulate the adult world around them. Instead of toys inspired by international conflict, manufacturers and parents wanted peaceful toys for their children to play with. Britains, the manufacturer who had been so successful in the production of toy soldiers before the war, shifted production to farms and animals, towns and cars, recognising there was no longer a commercial appetite for children's toys inspired by violence.

Children's literature also redefined its focus in the post-war years. Books for children became more clearly defined by age range. Schoolgirl fiction particularly settled into a style most suited for those aged 9–12, its themes exclusively concerned with the preoccupations of childhood.[8] No longer were girls' fictional heroines likely to be young women; instead, they were much more likely to be schoolgirls themselves. During the war itself girls' fiction had, like the fiction aimed at boys, tried to give children a sense of the adult world of war. Wartime fictional heroines drove ambulances and military vehicles, worked in munitions factories and caught spies; but they also took care of their appearance, made chutney and fell in love. While this shows some indication of an acknowledgement that women were capable of more than just domestic duties, it hardly suggests that women writers of girls' fiction were hoping to revolutionise the outlook and prospects of their readership.

Wartime toys aimed at girls had also maintained a focus on traditional female roles. They may have been excluded from the military games produced for their brothers, but there were nurses' uniforms and toy hospitals to amuse girls. They were encouraged to tend the soldiers that fell in their brothers' battles but not to want to play with them. The war encouraged the production of toys and the creation of games sharply divided along gender lines. Masculinity became closely associated with soldiering, just as femininity did with domestic roles and nursing.

But opportunities for girls to become more involved in life outside the home had been opened up by the war. As Guides, they served in public buildings and hospitals, raising the profile of young women and proving their capabilities. Despite state and public recognition of this service, the emphasis for Guides remained traditional. Girls needed to be trained to be useful companions to men, taught homecraft and hygiene so that they could fulfil their biological destiny as wives and mothers to the future sons of empire. Youth groups like the Girl Guides, Scouts and Boys' Brigade were set up in the pre-war years to answer adult anxieties about the development of sufficient moral character in working-class adolescents. They became immensely popular because they successfully combined their emphasis on character training with adventurous activities that children enjoyed.

For the leaders of Britain's uniformed youth groups there was no question that the war was necessary. In fact, war was held up as an ideal example of what happens to a country if its citizens do not take responsibility for the security of the nation. Despite denying any links to the country's military machine, the leaders of Britain's male uniformed youth groups saw their organisations as the ideal way to instil in young men the desire to fight to defend their country. Indeed, we have seen how Robert Baden-Powell, founder of the Boy Scout movement, lamented the fact that he had not begun his movement earlier so that there would have been a body of trained men ready and willing to take up arms when war was declared.[9]

These organisations grew in popularity during the war partly because of the opportunities they offered young people to participate officially in the war effort. The Scouts and Guides particularly remained incredibly popular in the inter-war period, partly because they were able to broaden their focus from service to home and empire towards international brotherhood and class harmony, so central to the politics of the 1920s and 1930s. After the war, Guides and Scouts continued to represent the best of British youth, functioning as a 'living memorial to the fallen and as a public reminder of the resilience of youth'.[10] Service remained at the core of these movements, but the focus shifted from national emergency to regeneration.

Children were central to this emphasis on regeneration both during the war and after it. The war had placed children at the heart of the debate about Britain's future – it was no longer enough to talk about 'national efficiency' and bemoan the lack of interest in the empire. If war was to be avoided in the future, and if Britain was to remain a strong imperial power, children must be educated both intellectually and morally for the task ahead. Attention had been focused on the education and training of young people in the pre-war years by philanthropists, labour and trade union leaders, imperialists and educators. There was concern over the security of the British Empire in the light of the falling birth rate and poor standards of health and education amongst the working population. Children were seen as a hope for the future, a way of ensuring that Britain could continue to compete in both trade and war. So, just as pre-war legislation sought to protect children's health and well being in order that they might be fit to serve their country in years to come, so their minds and moral development became a focus to ensure that children understood and accepted this future responsibility.

The war helped propel the education debate to the forefront of British politics. There was shock at the deficiencies in the curriculum, which had left British industry weak in comparison with Germany, and fears over the wastage of young people who had left school early to support the wartime economy. Educationalists, socialists and now industrialists too argued for greater attention to be paid to the schooling of working-class children in order to supply a better-educated workforce to compete internationally with both military and trade rivals.[11] Increased spending on education was now not only a priority but a necessity, and campaigners hoped for a bill that would see government involve itself in every stage of education and introduce truly progressive measures to ensure a workforce fit to rebuild the country after the ravages of war. Despite the significant financial cutbacks to the 1918 Education Act made in the 1920s, its priorities continued to dominate the education debate until after the Second World War.

And what of the children themselves? What was growing up during the war actually like? How did children respond to their lessons at school and the instructions of their youth group leaders? How did they understand the war, and what place did it have in their imaginations? What did it feel like not to know when they might see their fathers and brothers again? From the evidence collected here, it appears that children relished the chance to become involved with the war effort and learn about it at school. When given the chance, children enthusiastically collected, saved and made things for the war. They earned badges, certificates and the praise of their teachers for their work and seemed to want to genuinely be a part of the national endeavour whenever they could. Children tried, just like the adults around them, to help win the war. They believed in its message of crusade, were fearful for the future if defeated, and believed that they could make a difference.[12] Children's mobilisation for war was complete because they absorbed the messages delivered by adults through their lessons, youth groups, books and toys, but appropriated them for use in their own private relationships, fantasy and play.

Notes

1 Introduction

1. B.C. Brown, *Southwards from Swiss Cottage* (London: 1947) pp. 28–9.
2. A.L. Rowse, *A Cornish Childhood – Autobiography of a Cornishman* (London: 1942) p. 97.
3. Jay Winter, *The Great War and the British People* (Basingstoke: 2003) p. 28.
4. Stéphane Audoin-Rouzeau and Annette Becker, *1914–1918: Understanding the Great War*, trans. Catherine Temerson (London: 2002) p. 102.
5. Ibid.
6. Alan Kramer, 'Combatants and Noncombatants: Atrocities, Massacres and War Crimes,' in *A Companion to World War 1*, ed. John Horne (2010).
7. Audoin-Rouzeau and Becker, *1914–1918: Understanding the Great War* p. 103.
8. Ibid., p. 3.
9. Annette Becker, 'Faith, Ideologies, and the "Cultures of War",' in *A Companion to World War 1*, ed. John Horne (2010), p. 236.
10. Audoin-Rouzeau and Becker, *1914–1918: Understanding the Great War* p. 114.
11. Ibid., p. 110.
12. Ibid., p. 112.
13. Ibid., p. 111.
14. Stéphane Audoin-Rouzeau, 'Children and the Primary Schools of France, 1914–1918,' in *State Society and Mobilization in Europe During the First World War*, ed. John Horne (Cambridge: 1997), pp. 48–9.
15. Ibid., p. 52.
16. Andrea Fava, 'War, "National Education" and the Italian Primary School, 1915–1918,' in *State Society and Mobilization in Europe During the First World War*, ed. John Horne (Cambridge: 1997), p. 63.
17. Ibid.
18. Ibid., p. 61.
19. Susan R. Fisher, *Boys and Girls in No Man's Land – English-Canadian Children and the First World War* (Toronto: 2011) pp. 256–7.
20. George L. Mosse, *Fallen Soldiers – Reshaping the Memory of the World Wars* (Oxford: 1990) pp. 137–42.
21. Ibid., p. 143.
22. Fisher, *Boys and Girls in No Man's Land – English-Canadian Children and the First World War* p. 25.
23. Mosse, *Fallen Soldiers – Reshaping the Memory of the World Wars* p. 11.
24. Ibid., p. 159.
25. Pierre Purseigle, 'Introduction,' in *Warfare and Belligerence – Perspectives in First World War Studies*, ed. Pierre Purseigle (2005), p. 6.
26. Winter, *The Great War and the British People* p. 140.
27. Deborah Dwork, *War Is Good for Babies and Other Young Children – a History of the Infant and Child Welfare Movement in England 1898–1918* (London: 1987) p. 211.

28. Ibid., p. 209.
29. Harry Hendrick, 'Child Labour, Medical Capital and the School Medical Service, 1890–1918,' in *In the Name of the Child – Health and Welfare, 1880–1940*, ed. Roger Cooter (London: 1992), p. 49.
30. Hugh Cunningham, *Children and Childhood in Western Society since 1500* (London: 1995) pp. 165–69.
31. Arthur Marwick, *The Deluge – British Society and the First World War*, 2nd ed. (London: 1991) p. 43.
32. Anna Davin, *Growing up Poor – Home, School and Street in London 1870–1914* (London: 1996) p. 2.
33. The one other group largely excluded from the book are infants, due to the lack of appropriate evidence through which to reconstruct their experience.
34. Carolyn Steedman, *Dust* (Manchester: 2001) p. 76.
35. Carolyn Steedman, *Past Tenses – Essays on Writing, Autobiography and History* (London: 1992) p. 12.
36. Carolyn Steedman, *Strange Dislocations – Childhood and the Idea of Human Interiority, 1780–1930* (Cambridge, MA: 1995) p. 4.
37. Graham Dawson, *Soldier Heroes – British Adventure, Empire and the Imagining of Masculinities* (London: 1994) p. 241.
38. Ibid., p. 1.
39. Ibid., p. 241.
40. Ilana Bet-El, *Conscripts. Forgotten Men of the Great War* (Stroud: 2003) p. 135.
41. Martha Hanna, *Your Death Would Be Mine – Paul and Marie Pireaud in the Great War* (London: 2006), Christa Hämmerle, ' "You Let a Weeping Woman Call You Home?" Private Correspondences During the First World War in Austria and Germany,' in *Epistolary Selves: Letters and Letter-Writers, 1600–1945*, ed. Rebecca Earle (Aldershot: 1999), Michael Roper, *The Secret Battle – Emotional Survival in the Great War* (Manchester: 2009).
42. Hanna, *Your Death Would Be Mine – Paul and Marie Pireaud in the Great War* p. 288.
43. Martha Hanna, 'A Republic of Letters: The Epistolary Tradition in France During World War 1,' *The American Historical Review* 108, no. 5 (2003): para 8.
44. Ibid.
45. Roper, *The Secret Battle – Emotional Survival in the Great War* p. 266.
46. Ibid.
47. Nicholas Mosley, *Julian Grenfell – His Life and the Times of His Death 1888–1915* (London: 1999) p. 358.
48. Peter Parker, *The Old Lie – the Great War and the Public School Ethos* (London: 1987) p. 17.
49. James Walvin, *A Child's World – a Social History of English Childhood 1800–1914*. Harmondsworth: Penguin, 1982.
50. Sally Mitchell, *The New Girl – Girls Culture in England 1880–1915* (New York: 1995) p. 137.
51. Ibid., p. 3.
52. John MacKenzie, *Propaganda and Empire – the Manipulation of British Public Opinion, 1880–1960* (Manchester: 1984) p. 176.
53. Ibid., p. 181.
54. See John Springhall, *Youth, Empire and Society – British Youth Movements, 1883–1940* (London: 1977) and Michael Rosenthal, *The Character Factory – Baden Powell and the Origins of the Boy Scout Movement* (London: 1986).

55. Mitchell, *The New Girl – Girls Culture in England 1880–1915* p. 126.
56. Gerard J. DeGroot, *Blighty – British Society in the Era of the Great War* (London: 1996) p. 39.
57. Ibid., p. 40.
58. Ian Beckett, 'The Nation in Arms, 1914–1918,' in *A Nation in Arms*, ed. Ian Beckett and Keith Simpson (Manchester: 1985), p. 5.
59. DeGroot, *Blighty – British Society in the Era of the Great War* p. 40.
60. Winter, *The Great War and the British People* p. 274. Actual figure 355, 211, p. 71.
61. Becker, 'Faith, Ideologies, and the "Cultures of War",' p. 236.

2   Families at War

1. M. Keen, *Childhood Memories 1903–1921*, Working Class Autobiographical Archive – Brunel University (London) p. 27.
2. E. Hall, *Canary Girls and Stockpots* (Luton: 1977) p. 10.
3. Ibid., p. 6.
4. A.P. Jacobs, *Just Take a Look at These*, Working Class Autobiographical Archive – Brunel University (London) unpaginated.
5. Ibid.
6. Ulrich Trumpener, 'The Turkish War, 1914–18,' in *A Companion to World War 1*, ed. John Horne (Wiley-Blackwell: 2010), p. 103.
7. J.H. Armitage, *The Twenty Three Years. Or the Late Way of Life and of Living*, Working Class Autobiographical Archive – Brunel University (London) p. 59.
8. Erika Kuhlman, *Of Little Comfort: War Widows, Fallen Soldiers, and the Remaking of the Nation after the Great War* (New York University Press: 2012) p. 5.
9. Armitage, *The Twenty Three Years. Or the Late Way of Life and of Living*, p. 60.
10. Ibid., p. 62.
11. Jay Winter, *The Great War and the British People* (Basingstoke: 2003) p. 38.
12. C.H. Rolph, *London Particulars* (Oxford: 1980) p. 176.
13. Jay Winter, *The Experience of World War 1* (London: 1988).
14. Rolph, *London Particulars* p. 176.
15. Jacobs, *Just Take a Look at These* unpaginated.
16. Peter Boyden, *Tommy Atkins' Letters – the History of the British Army Postal Service from 1795* (London: 1990) p. 30 and Edward Wells, *Mailshot: A History of the Forces Postal Service* (London: 1987) p. 64.
17. Joanna Bourke, *Dismembering the Male: Men's Bodies, Britain and the Great War* (London: 1996), Helen B. McCartney, *Citizen Soldiers – the Liverpool Territorials in the First World War* (Cambridge: 2005) and Martha Hanna, *Your Death Would Be Mine – Paul and Marie Pireaud in the Great War* (London: 2006).
18. Boyden, *Tommy Atkins' Letters – the History of the British Army Postal Service from 1795* p. 30.
19. McCartney, *Citizen Soldiers – the Liverpool Territorials in the First World War* p. 91.
20. Michael Roper, *The Secret Battle – Emotional Survival in the Great War* (Manchester: 2009) p. 51.
21. Ibid., p. 63.

22. In Germany letters sent out to troops were liable to be censored. Wives complaining too bitterly about conditions on the home front sometimes had their letters returned by the Army as they were considered too dangerous to troop morale. Christa Hämmerle, ' "You Let a Weeping Woman Call You Home?" Private Correspondences During the First World War in Austria and Germany', in *Epistolary Selves: Letters and Letter-Writers, 1600–1945*, ed. Rebecca Earle (Aldershot: 1999), pp. 154–7.
23. Ibid., pp. 158–9.
24. P. Fussell, *The Great War and Modern Memory* (Oxford: 1975) p. 185.
25. Ibid.
26. File references for each set of correspondents are included in the bibliography.
27. Bourke, *Dismembering the Male: Men's Bodies, Britain and the Great War* p. 23.
28. Fussell, *The Great War and Modern Memory* p. 181.
29. C. Isherwood, *Exhumation* (London: 1966) p. 170.
30. Ibid.
31. Ibid.
32. Ibid., p. 171.
33. Joanna Bourke, *An Intimate History of Killing – Face to Face Killing in Twentieth Century Warfare* (London: 1999) p. 13.
34. Ibid., p. 42.
35. Michael Roper, 'Maternal Relations: Moral Manliness and Emotional Survival in Letters Home During the First World War', in *Masculinities in Politics and War – Gendering Modern History*, ed. Stefan Dudink, Karen Hagemann and John Tosh (Manchester: 2004), p. 308.

3 War Imagined

1. C.H. Rolph, *London Particulars* (Oxford: 1980), p. 126.
2. Ibid., p. 123.
3. Kenneth D. Brown, *The British Toy Business – A History since 1700* (London: 1996), p. 56.
4. Ibid., p. 64.
5. Ibid., p. 78.
6. Leslie Daiken, *Children's Toys Throughout the Ages* (London: Spring Books, 1963), p. 137.
7. Antonia Fraser, *A History of Toys* (London: 1966), p. 231.
8. Ibid.
9. Graham Dawson, *Soldier Heroes – British Adventure, Empire and the Imagining of Masculinities* (London: 1994), p. 239.
10. Ibid.
11. Hanna Segal, *Klein* (Brighton: 1979), p. 36.
12. D.W. Winnicott, *Playing and Reality* (London: 1971), p. 51.
13. Ibid., p. 100.
14. Kenneth D. Brown, 'Modelling for War? Toy Soldiers in Late Victorian and Edwardian Britain', *Journal of Social History* 24, no. 2 (1990).
15. Ibid., p. 238.
16. Ibid., p. 239.

17. H.G. Wells, *Little Wars* (London: 1913), p. 7.
18. Ibid., p. 97.
19. Ibid., p. 100.
20. Ibid., p. 101.
21. Nicola Johnson, 'Penny Plain, Tuppence Coloured', in *Patriotism: The Making and Unmaking of British National Identity, Vol 3: National Fictions*, ed. Raphael Samuel (London: 1989), p. 254.
22. Henry Harris, *Model Soldiers* (London: 1962), p. 34.
23. Richard Church, *Over the Bridge – An Essay in Autobiography* (London: 1955), p. 169.
24. Fraser, *A History of Toys*, p. 231.
25. H.G. Wells, *Floor Games* (London: 1911), p. 22.
26. *The Toy and Fancy Goods Trader*, February 1914.
27. A.J. Holladay, *War Games for Boy Scouts – Played with Model Soldiers* (London: 1910), p. 2.
28. *Games and Toys*, November 1914.
29. Ibid.
30. Ibid.
31. Evelyn Waugh, *A Little Learning – The First Volume of an Autobiography* (London: 1964), p. 59.
32. Ibid.
33. Rev. J. Leonard Smith, *A Tansley Boyhood* (Loughborough: 1996), p. 45.
34. Ibid.
35. *Games and Toys*, September 1915.
36. Nicholas Whittaker, *Toys Were Us – A History of Twentieth Century Toys and Toy-Making* (London: 2001), p. 22.
37. *Games and Toys*, March 1915.
38. Peter Johnson, *Toy Armies* (London: 1981), p. 55.
39. *Little Folks*, September 1917.
40. M. Keen, *Childhood Memories 1903–1921*, Working Class Autobiographical Archive – Brunel University (London), p. 26.
41. James Walvin, *A Child's World – A Social History of English Childhood 1800–1914* (Harmondsworth: 1982), and Peter Parker, *The Old Lie – The Great War and the Public School Ethos* (London: 1987).
42. Mary Cadogan and Patricia Craig, *Women and Children First – The Fiction of Two World Wars* (London: 1978), p. 31.
43. Kelly Boyd, *Manliness and the Boys' Story Paper in Britain: A Cultural History, 1855–1940* (Basingstoke: 2003), p. 98.
44. Cadogan and Craig, *Women and Children First – The Fiction of Two World Wars*, p. 72.
45. Capt. F.S. Brereton, *With French at the Front – A Story of the Great War Down to the Battle of the Aisne* (1915), p. 40.
46. Capt. F.S. Brereton, *Under Haig in Flanders – A Story of Vimy, Messines and Ypres* (Acquired by the British Museum, 1918), p. 57.
47. Ibid., p. 163.
48. Ibid., p. 58.
49. Ibid., p. 63.
50. P.F. Westerman, *The Fritz Strafers – A Story of the Great War* (London: Acquired by the British Museum 1919), p. 297.

51. Angela Brazil, *The School by the Sea* (Acquired by the British Museum 1914), p. 13.
52. Brereton, *With French at the Front – A Story of the Great War Down to the Battle of the Aisne*, p. 48.
53. Brenda Girvin, *Munition Mary* (1918), p. 281.
54. Bessie Marchant, *A Transport Girl in France* (Acquired by the British Museum 1919), p. 81.
55. Sally Mitchell, *The New Girl – Girls Culture in England 1880–1915* (New York: 1995), pp. 121–6.
56. Geoffrey Whitworth, *The Child's ABC of the War* (London: 1914).
57. *Our Soldiers – An ABC for Little Britons* (London: 1916).
58. *The Royal Navy – An ABC for Little Britons* (London: 1915).
59. Nina MacDonald, *War-Time Nursery Rhymes* (London: Acquired by the British Museum 1919), p. 6.
60. Ibid., p. 13.
61. Charlotte Schaller, *At War!* (London: 1917), p. 30.
62. James Thirsk, *A Beverley Child's Great War* (Beverley: 2000), p. 25.
63. Brown, 'Modelling for War? Toy Soldiers in Late Victorian and Edwardian Britain' and Walvin, *A Child's World – A Social History of English Childhood 1800–1914*.

4   Children in Uniform

1. Charles Booth, *Life and Labour of the People in London* (London: 1889), Seebohm Rowntree, *Poverty, a Study of Town Life* (London: 1901).
2. Peter Parker, *The Old Lie – the Great War and the Public School Ethos* (London: 1987).
3. Anna Davin, 'Imperialism and Motherhood,' *History Workshop Journal* 5 (1978), Sally Mitchell, *The New Girl – Girls Culture in England 1880–1915* (New York: 1995).
4. Michael J. Childs, *Labour's Apprentices – Working Class Lads in Late Victorian and Edwardian England* (London 1992). And Stephen Humphries, *Hooligans or Rebels?: An Oral History of Working-Class Childhood and Youth 1889–1939* (Oxford: 1981).
5. John Springhall, Brian Fraser and Michael Hoare, *Sure and Steadfast – a History of the Boys' Brigade 1883 to 1983* (London: 1983) p. 26.
6. Booth, *Life and Labour of the People in London*.
7. For further discussion on fears for the future of the empire and formation of Scouts and Guides, see Tammy M. Proctor, 'On My Honour – Guides and Scouts in Interwar Britain,' *Transactions of the American Philosophical Society* 92, no. 2 (2002).
8. John Springhall, *Youth, Empire and Society – British Youth Movements, 1883–1940* (London: 1977) p. 22.
9. Springhall, Fraser and Hoare, *Sure and Steadfast – A History of the Boys' Brigade 1883 to 1983*, p. 258.
10. Ibid., p. 26.
11. John Tosh, 'Hegemonic Masculinity and the History of Gender,' in *Masculinities in Politics and War – Gendering Modern History*, ed. Stefan Dudink, Karen Hagemann and John Tosh (Manchester: 2004), p. 55.

12. The Boys' Brigade, *The Boys' Brigade Gazette*, February (1891), pp. 168–9.
13. Springhall, *Youth, Empire and Society – British Youth Movements, 1883–1940*, p. 45.
14. Ibid. and Michael Rosenthal, *The Character Factory – Baden Powell and the Origins of the Boy Scout Movement* (London: 1986). Tim Jeal, *Baden-Powell* (London: 1991).
15. Springhall, *Youth, Empire and Society – British Youth Movements, 1883–1940*, p. 57.
16. Ibid., p. 59.
17. Rosenthal, *The Character Factory – Baden Powell and the Origins of the Boy Scout Movement*, p. 102.
18. Allen Warren, 'Sir Robert Baden-Powell, the Scout Movement and Citizen Training in Great Britain, 1900–1920,' *English Historical Review* 101 (1986). Martin Dedman, 'Baden-Powell, Militarism, and the "Invisible Contributors" to the Boy Scout Scheme, 1904–1920,' *Twentieth Century British History*, 4, no. 3 (1993), and Proctor, 'On My Honour – Guides and Scouts in Interwar Britain.'
19. Exceptions to this include Proctor, 'On My Honour – Guides and Scouts in Interwar Britain.'
20. Alan Penn, *Targeting Schools – Drill, Militarism and Imperialism* (London: 1999).
21. Ibid., p. 147.
22. Rosenthal, *The Character Factory – Baden Powell and the Origins of the Boy Scout Movement*, p. 162.
23. Alwyn Dawson, *The Story of the 1st Chiswick – Early Years 1908–1939* (1978), p. 15.
24. John R. Hughes, *Thirty Years and More* (Derby: 1996), p. 15.
25. John Springhall, 'The Boy Scouts, Class and Militarism in Relation to British Youth Movements 1883–1935,' *International Review of Social History* 16, no. 2 (1971), p. 138.
26. Lord Milner quoted in The Irish Scout Association, *The Irish Scout Gazette*, February 1921.
27. Springhall, *Youth, Empire and Society – British Youth Movements, 1883–1940*, p. 111.
28. Ibid., p. 114.
29. Ibid., pp. 117–18.
30. Springhall, Fraser and Hoare, *Sure and Steadfast – a History of the Boys' Brigade 1883 to 1983*, p. 258. And Springhall, *Youth, Empire and Society – British Youth Movements, 1883–1940*, p. 134.
31. The Boys' Brigade, *The Boys' Brigade Gazette*, October 1914, p. 20.
32. The Boy Scout Association, *Headquarters Gazette*, August 1914, p. 233.
33. The Boy Scout Association, *The Scout*, August 1914.
34. Streatham Sea Scout Association, *Golden Jubilee of the 4th Streatham Sea Scout Group. 1913–1963* (London: 1963), p. 1.
35. The Boy Scout Association, *Headquarters Gazette*, p. 233.
36. Ibid., p. 262.
37. Ibid.
38. Ibid., p. 80.
39. Ibid., p. 262.

40. Alec J. Spalding, *The 24th, 1908–1988 – a History of the 24th Glasgow (Bearsden) Scout Group* (1988), p. 11.
41. Dawson, *The Story of the 1st Chiswick – Early Years 1908–1939*, p. 18.
42. The Boy Scout Association, *Headquarters Gazette*, p. 263.
43. John F Rickard, *Scouting around Portishead* (2000), p. 30.
44. The Boy Scout Association, *Headquarters Gazette*, p. 263.
45. Ibid., p. 290.
46. Ibid., p. 321.
47. Ibid., p. 290.
48. Ibid., p. 291.
49. Ibid., p. 347.
50. By the end of the war 25,000 Scouts had served on coastguard duty and 80,000 had earned their War Service badges. More than 100,000 Scouts, former Scouts and Scoutmasters became soldiers in the conflict, 10,000 of whom died in combat. The Boy Scout Association, *11th Annual Report* (London, 1919), pp. 15–17.
51. The Boy Scout Association, *Headquarters Gazette*, May 1916, p. 115.
52. Ibid.
53. The Boys' Brigade, *Boys' Brigade Gazette*, June 1917, p. 114.
54. Springhall, Fraser and Hoare, *Sure and Steadfast – a History of the Boys' Brigade 1883 to 1983*, p. 116.
55. Dedman, 'Baden-Powell, Militarism, and the "Invisible Contributors" to the Boy Scout Scheme, 1904–1920,' p. 218.
56. By April 1918 the Boys' Brigade had issued 2,650 badges for boys who gave over 100 hours' unpaid and voluntary service outside school or work hours.
57. Robert Baden-Powell, *Girl Guides: A Suggestion for Character Training for Girls* (London: 1909), p. 7.
58. Ibid., p. 9.
59. Ibid.
60. Ibid.
61. Rose Kerr and Alex Liddell, *The Story of the Girl Guides 1908–1938* (London: 1976), p. 30.
62. Ibid., p. 34.
63. Ibid., p. 38.
64. Ibid., p. 36.
65. Ibid., p. 112.
66. Ibid., p. 38.
67. Proctor, 'On My Honour – Guides and Scouts in Interwar Britain,' p. 25.
68. Girl Guide Association, *Girl Guide Gazette*, August 1914.
69. Joan Warrack and Peggy Greening, *Girl Guides – the Edinburgh Story* (Edinburgh: 1977), p. 119.
70. Girl Guide Association, *Girl Guide Gazette*, October 1915.
71. Ibid.
72. Ibid.
73. Girl Guide Association, *Annual Report* (London, 1916), p. 3.
74. Proctor, 'On My Honour – Guides and Scouts in Interwar Britain,' p. 109.
75. Olave Baden-Powell, *Training Girls as Guides* (London: 1917), p. 22.
76. Proctor, 'On My Honour – Guides and Scouts in Interwar Britain,' p. 109.

77. Richard A. Voeltz, ' "The Antidote to Khaki Fever"? – the Expansion of the British Girl Guides During the First World War,' *Journal of Contemporary History* 27, no. 4 (1992).
78. Carol Dyhouse, *Girls Growing up in Late Victorian and Edwardian England* (London: 1981), p. 113.
79. Voeltz, ' "The Antidote to Khaki Fever"? – the Expansion of the British Girl Guides During the First World War.'
80. Ibid., p. 633.
81. Ibid.
82. Girl Guide Association, *Annual Report*, p. 14.
83. Davin, 'Imperialism and Motherhood.'
84. Girl Guide Association, *Annual Report*, p. 15.
85. Allen Warren, ' "Mothers for the Empire"? – the Girl Guide Association in Britain, 1909–1939,' in *Making Imperial Mentalities – Socialisation and British Imperialism*, ed. J. A. Mangan (Manchester: 1990), p. 108.
86. Proctor, 'On My Honour – Guides and Scouts in Interwar Britain,' p. 72.

5 War in the Classroom

1. John Graves, *Policy and Progress in Secondary Education 1902–1942* (London, 1943), p. 110.
2. Peter Gordon, Richard Aldrich and Dennis Dean, *Education and Policy in England in the Twentieth Century* (London, 1991), p. 278.
3. Keith Evans, *The Development and Structure of the English School System* (London, 1985), p. 84. Peter Gordon and Denis Lawton, *Curriculum Change in the Nineteenth and Twentieth Centuries* (London, 1978), pp. 59–60.
4. Herbert Cornish, ed., *The Code for Public Elementary Schools 1904–5*, vol. VI, *The School Government Handbooks* (London, 1904), p. 11.
5. Peter Cunningham, 'Primary Education,' in *A Century of Education*, ed. Richard Aldrich (London, 2002), p. 14.
6. Board of Education, *Handbook of Suggestions for the Consideration of Teachers and Others Concerned with the Work of the Public Elementary Schools* (London, 1905), pp. 14–15.
7. Gordon, Aldrich and Dean, *Education and Policy in England in the Twentieth Century*, p. 282.
8. Gary McCulloch, 'Secondary Education,' in *A Century of Education*, ed. Richard Aldrich (London, 2002), p. 36.
9. Brian Simon, *Education and the Labour Movement, 1870–1920* (London, 1974), p. 104.
10. Board of Education, 'Report of the Board of Education 1917–18,' (London, 1918), p. 13.
11. Geoffrey Sherington, *English Education, Social Change and War 1911–1920* (Manchester, 1981), p. 49.
12. S.J. Curtis, *History of Education in Great Britain* (London, 1967), p. 339.
13. Sherington, *English Education, Social Change and War 1911–1920*, p. 49.
14. Ministry of Reconstruction, 'Juvenile Employment During the War and After' (London, 1918), p. 49.
15. Sherington, *English Education, Social Change and War 1911–1920*, p. 50.

16. *The Schoolmaster*, 30 December 1916, p. 370.
17. Board of Education, 'Circular 944' (1916), p. 1.
18. Ibid., p. 2.
19. Ibid., p. 3.
20. Martin Pugh, *Women and the Women's Movement in Britain 1914–1959* (Basingstoke, 1992), pp. 19–21.
21. Board of Education, 'Circular 944,' p. 4.
22. Ibid., p. 6.
23. *The Schoolmaster*, 3 October 1914, p. 485.
24. Ibid.
25. Ibid.
26. Board of Education, *Handbook of Suggestions for the Consideration of Teachers and Others Concerned with the Work of the Public Elementary Schools*, p. 6.
27. Board of Education, 'Circular 869' (1914), p. 3.
28. Sir James Yoxall, *Why Britain Went to War – to the Boys and Girls of the British Empire* (London, 1914), p. 15.
29. Albert A. Cock, *A Syllabus in War Geography and History – for Use in Senior Classes in Elementary and Secondary Schools* (London, 1916), p. 31.
30. Ibid., p. 32.
31. Richard Wilson, *The First Year of the Great War – Being the Story of the First Phase of the Great World Struggle for Honour, Justice and Truth. Told for Boys and Girls of the British Empire* (London, 1916), pp. 8–9.
32. H.W. Household, *Our Sea Power – Its Story and Meaning* (London, 1918), foreword.
33. Christopher Martin, *A Short History of English Schools 1750–1965* (Hove, 1979), p. 80.
34. M. Cowley, *My Daddy Is a Soldier: A Working Class Family in the Lloyd George Era*, Local Studies Collection – Richmond upon Thames, p. 10.
35. Ibid., p. 11.
36. Ibid., p. 21.
37. Ibid., pp. 21–2.
38. C. Gasquoine Hartley and Arthur D. Lewis, *Children of the Empire – a Young Citizens Reader* (London, 1916), p. 10.
39. Ibid., p. 94.
40. Board of Education, 'Board of Education Annual Report 1914–1915' (London, 1915), pp. 11–12.
41. Ibid.
42. Ibid., p. 13.
43. File references for each set of correspondents are included in the bibliography.
44. Panikos Panayi, *The Enemy in Our Midst: Germans in Britain During the First World War* (Oxford, 1991).
45. Home leave was not possible for Australian soldiers, and even the post they received took at least 50 days to arrive; Joy Damousi, *The Labour of Loss. Mourning, Memory and Wartime Bereavement in Australia* (Cambridge, 1999), p. 19.
46. London County Council, 'Annual Report of the Council – Education, 1915–1919' (1920), p. 4.
47. Stuart Maclure, *A History of Education in London, 1870–1990* (London, 1990), pp. 83–96.

48. Ibid., p. 86.
49. London County Council, 'Annual Report of the Council – Education, 1915–1919,' p. 5.
50. Ibid., p. 6.
51. 'Our School War Record.'
52. 'School Magazine,' December 1915.
53. 'Log Book.'
54. London County Council, 'Annual Report of the Council – Education, 1915–1919,' p. 8.
55. Ibid., p. 5.
56. Ibid., p. 9.
57. Ibid., p. 7.
58. London County Council, 'Air Raids' (1917), p. 2.
59. Ibid., p. 3.
60. London County Council, 'Air Raids in School Time' (1917).
61. Gerard J. DeGroot, *Blighty – British Society in the Era of the Great War* (London, 1996), pp. 214–18.
62. Anna Davin, 'Imperialism and Motherhood,' *History Workshop Journal* 5 (1978).
63. London County Council, 'Annual Report of the Council – Education, 1915–1919,' p. 11.
64. Ibid.
65. Cowley, *My Daddy Is a Soldier: A Working Class Family in the Lloyd George Era*, p. 73.
66. Arthur Marwick, *The Deluge – British Society and the First World War*, 2nd ed. (London: 1991), p. 198.
67. Susan Grayzel, *At Home and under Fire – Air Raids and Culture in Britain from the Great War to the Blitz* (2012).
68. K. Betterton, *'White Pinnies, Black Aprons ...'*, Working Class Autobiographical Archive – Brunel University (London), p. 24.
69. A.P. Jacobs, *Just Take a Look at These*, Working Class Autobiographical Archive – Brunel University (London).
70. Ibid.
71. *The Schoolmaster*, 25 December 1915, p. 906.
72. 'The Schoolmaster' 30 December 1916, p. 800.
73. Ibid.
74. Ibid., p. 800.
75. London County Council, 'Annual Report of the Council – Education, 1915–1919,' pp. 11–12.
76. Martin, *A Short History of English Schools 1750–1965*, p. 87.

6 Conclusion

1. Tammy Proctor, *Civilians in a World at War, 1914–1918* (New York: New York University Press, 2010), p. 7.
2. A.L. Rowse, *A Cornish Childhood – Autobiography of a Cornishman* (London, 1942), p. 188.
3. Martha Hanna, *Your Death Would Be Mine – Paul and Marie Pireaud in the Great War* (London, 2006), Christa Hämmerle, ' "You Let a Weeping Woman Call

You Home?" Private Correspondences During the First World War in Austria and Germany,' in *Epistolary Selves: Letters and Letter-Writers, 1600–1945*, ed. Rebecca Earle (Aldershot, 1999), Michael Roper, *The Secret Battle – Emotional Survival in the Great War* (Manchester, 2009).

4. Susan Kingsley Kent, *Making Peace – The Reconstruction of Gender in Interwar Britain* (Princeton, 1993), p. 99.

5. Gail Braybon and Penny Summerfield, *Out of the Cage: Women's Experiences in Two World Wars* (London, 1987). Kent, *Making Peace – the Reconstruction of Gender in Interwar Britain*.

6. Ibid.

7. Stéphane Audoin-Rouzeau and Annette Becker, *1914–1918: Understanding the Great War*, trans. Catherine Temerson (London, 2002), p. 102.

8. Sally Mitchell, *The New Girl – Girls Culture in England 1880–1915* (New York: 1995), p. 173.

9. The Boy Scout Association, *Headquarters Gazette*, September (1914), p. 263.

10. Tammy M. Proctor, 'On My Honour – Guides and Scouts in Interwar Britain,' *Transactions of the American Philosophical Society*, 92, no. 2 (2002), p. 156.

11. Peter Gordon, Richard Aldrich and Dennis Dean, *Education and Policy in England in the Twentieth Century* (London, 1991), p. 35. And Peter Gordon, 'Curriculum,' in *A Century of Education*, ed. Richard Aldrich (London, 2002), p. 192.

12. Annette Becker, 'Faith, Ideologies, and the "Cultures of War",' in *A Companion to World War 1*, ed. John Horne (Oxford: Wiley-Blackwell, 2010).

Bibliography

Primary sources

Archival sources

London Metropolitan Archives

Board of Education. 'Circulars.' Nos. 816 to 1081 (1913–1918). (LCC/EO/GEN/10/13)

London County Council. 'Annual Report of the Council – Education, 1915–1919.' 1920 (LCC Official Publications)

London County Council. 'Miscellaneous Printed Reports.' (EO/GEN/5/34)

London County Council. 'Air Raids.' 1917. (EO/WAR/3/1)

London County Council. 'Air Raids in School Time.' 1917. (EO/WAR/3/1)

Brecknock School. 'Log Book.' (EO/DIV2/BRE/LB/1)

Cobourg Road School. 'Our School War Record.' (EO/PS/11/58)

Wood Close School. 'School Magazine.' (EO/PS/11/18)

Imperial War Museum

H. Bearer (Documents 6999)

E.G. Buckeridge (Documents 13267)

G. and E. Butling (Documents 2423)

I. Finn (Documents 9049)

J.B. Foulis (Documents 3563)

F.H. Gautier (Documents 2296)

J. Hancock (Documents 8146)

R.P. Harker (Documents 746)

H.N. Hignett (Documents 4817)

E. Hopkinson MC (Documents 2628)

Mrs D.C. MacDonald (née Tickner) (Documents 12297)

A.C. Stanton (Documents 7823)

W. Vernon (Documents 12771)

E.I. Williams (Documents 4337)

P.A. Wise (Documents 1131)

Reports

Board of Education. 'Board of Education Annual Report 1914–1915.' London: HMSO, 1915.

Board of Education. 'Report of the Board of Education 1917–18.' London: HMSO, 1918.

Girl Guide Association. 'Annual Report.' London, 1916.
Ministry of Reconstruction. 'Juvenile Employment During the War and After.' London: HMSO, 1918.
The Boy Scout Association. '11th Annual Report.' London, 1919.

Contemporary magazines and journals

Boys' Own Paper
Games and Toys
Girl Guide Gazette
Headquarters Gazette
Little Folks
The Boys' Brigade Gazette
The Scout
The Schoolmaster
The Toy and Fancy Goods Trader

Unpublished autobiography

All held in the Working Class Autobiographical Archive at Brunel University unless otherwise stated.
Armitage, J.H. 'The Twenty Three Years. Or the Late Way of Life and of Living.' (ref. 2–15)
Betterton, K. ' "White Pinnies, Black Aprons ...." ' (ref. 2–71)
Cowley, M. 'My Daddy Is a Soldier: A Working Class Family in the Lloyd George Era.' (Local Studies Collection – Richmond upon Thames, London).
Hannan, D.R. 'Those Happy Highways: An Autobiography.' (ref. 2–357)
Jacobs, A.P. 'Just Take a Look at These.' (ref. 2–431)
Keen, M. 'Childhood Memories 1903–1921.' (ref. 2–449)

Published autobiography

Brown, B.C. *Southwards from Swiss Cottage*. London: Home and Van Thal, 1947.
Church, Richard. *Over the Bridge – an Essay in Autobiography*. London: Heinemann, 1955.
Hall, E. *Canary Girls and Stockpots*. Luton: Workers Educational Association, 1977.
Isherwood, C. *Exhumation*. London: Methuen & Co. Ltd, 1966.
Rolph, C.H. *London Particulars*. Oxford: Oxford University Press, 1980.
Rowse, A.L. *A Cornish Childhood – Autobiography of a Cornishman*. London: Jonathan Cape, 1942.
Smith, Rev. J. Leonard. *A Tansley Boyhood*. Loughborough: Teamprint, 1996.
Thirsk, James. *A Beverley Child's Great War*. Beverley: Highgate Publications Ltd, 2000.
Waugh, Evelyn. *A Little Learning – the First Volume of an Autobiography*. London: Methuen & Co. Ltd, 1964.

Other published works

The Royal Navy – an ABC for Little Britons. London: Thomas Nelson, 1915.

Our Soldiers – an ABC for Little Britons. London: Thomas Nelson, 1916.

Baden-Powell, Olave. *Training Girls as Guides*. London: C. Arthur Pearson, 1917.

Baden-Powell, Robert. *Girl Guides: A Suggestion for Character Training for Girls*. London: Bishopsgate Press, 1909.

Board of Education. *Handbook of Suggestions for the Consideration of Teachers and Others Concerned with the Work of the Public Elementary Schools*. London: HMSO, 1905.

Brazil, Angela. *The School by the Sea*: Blackie and Son Ltd, Acquired by the British Museum, 1914.

Brereton, Capt. F.S. *With French at the Front – a Story of the Great War Down to the Battle of the Aisne*: Blackie and Son Ltd, 1915.

Brereton, Capt. F.S. *With Our Russian Allies*: Blackie and Son Ltd, 1916.

Brereton, Capt. F.S. *Under Haig in Flanders – a Story of Vimy, Messines and Ypres*: Blackie and Son Ltd, Acquired by the British Museum, 1918.

Bulkley. *The Feeding of School Children*. London: G. Bell, 1914.

Cock, Albert A. *A Syllabus in War Geography and History – for Use in Senior Classes in Elementary and Secondary Schools*. London: George Phillip and Son Ltd, 1916.

Cook, H. Caldwell. *The Play Way: An Essay in Educational Method*. Heinemann, 1917.

Girvin, Brenda. *Munition Mary*. Oxford University Press, 1918.

Hartley, C. Gasquoine and Arthur D. Lewis. *Children of the Empire – a Young Citizens Reader*. London: T Werner Laurie, 1916.

Holladay, A.J. *War Games for Boy Scouts – Played with Model Soldiers*. London: Gale & Polden, 1910.

Holmes, Edmond. *What Is and What Might Be: A Study of Education in General and Elementary Education in Particular*. London: Constable, 1911.

Household, H.W. *Our Sea Power – Its Story and Meaning*. London: Macmillan, 1918.

MacDonald, Nina. *War-Time Nursery Rhymes*. London: George Routledge and Sons, Acquired by the British Museum, 1919.

Marchant, Bessie. *A Transport Girl in France*. Blackie and Son Ltd, Acquired by the British Museum, 1919.

N.U.T. *War Record 1914–1919 – a Short Account of Duty and Work Accomplished During the War*. London: Hamilton House, 1920.

O'Neill, Elizabeth. *Battles for Peace: The Story of the Great War Told for Children*. London: Hodder and Stoughton, 1918.

Schaller, Charlotte. *At War!* London: Grant Richards, 1917.

Thorne, G. *The Secret Service Submarine – a Story of the Present War*: T.C. & E.C. Jack, 1915.

Wells, H.G. *Floor Games*. London: Frank Palmer, 1911.

Wells, H.G. *Little Wars*. London: Frank Palmer, 1913.

Westerman, P.F. *Rounding up the Raider – a Naval Story of the Great War*. London: Blackie and Son Ltd, Acquired by the British Museum, 1916.

Westerman, P.F. *The Fritz Strafers – a Story of the Great War*. London: S.W. Partridge & Co. Ltd., Acquired by the British Museum, 1919.

Whitworth, Geoffrey. *The Child's ABC of the War*. London: George Allen and Unwin Ltd, 1914.

Wilson, Richard. *The First Year of the Great War – Being the Story of the First Phase of the Great World Struggle for Honour, Justice and Truth. Told for Boys and Girls of the British Empire.* London: Chambers, 1916.

Wood, E. *How We Baffled the Germans – the Exciting Adventures of Two Boys in South West Africa.* Thomas Nelson & Son Ltd, Acquired by the British Museum, 1917.

Woodhouse, E. *What the Elephant Thinks of the Hun and Those 'out There', or, Jungle Jingles by Jumbo Junior for Other Little Juniors,* 1918.

Yoxall, Sir James. *Why Britain Went to War – to the Boys and Girls of the British Empire.* London: Cassell and Co., 1914.

Secondary sources

Journal articles and book chapters

Audoin-Rouzeau, Stéphane. 'Children and the Primary Schools of France, 1914–1918.' In *State Society and Mobilization in Europe During the First World War,* edited by John Horne. Cambridge: Cambridge University Press, 1997.

Becker, Annette. 'Faith, Ideologies, and the "Cultures of War".' In *A Companion to World War 1,* edited by John Horne. Wiley–Blackwell, 2010.

Beckett, Ian. 'The Nation in Arms, 1914–1918.' In *A Nation in Arms,* edited by Ian Beckett and Keith Simpson. Manchester: Manchester University Press, 1985.

Blanch, Michael. 'Imperialism, Nationalism and Organised Youth.' In *Working Class Culture – Studies in History and Theory,* edited by John Clarke, Chas Critcher and Richard Johnson. London: Hutchinson, 1979.

Brown, Kenneth D. 'Modelling for War? Toy Soldiers in Late Victorian and Edwardian Britain.' *Journal of Social History* 24, no. 2 (1990): 237–54.

Davin, Anna. 'Imperialism and Motherhood.' *History Workshop Journal* 5 (1978).

Dawson, Graham. 'The Blond Bedouin – Lawrence of Arabia, Imperial Adventure and the Imagining of English-British Masculinity.' In *Manful Assertions – Masculinities in Britain since 1800,* edited by Michael Roper and John Tosh. London: Routledge, 1991.

Deadman, Martin. 'Baden-Powell, Militarism, and the "Invisible Contributors" to the Boy Scout Scheme, 1904–1920.' *Twentieth Century British History* 4, no. 3 (1993): 201–23.

Fava, Andrea. 'War, "National Education" and the Italian Primary School, 1915–1918.' In *State Society and Mobilization in Europe During the First World War,* edited by John Horne. Cambridge: Cambridge University Press, 1997.

Gordon, Peter. 'The Handbook of Suggestions for Teachers: Its Origins and Evolution.' *Journal of Educational Administration and History* 17, no. 1 (1985): 41–8.

Gordon, Peter. 'Curriculum.' In *A Century of Education,* edited by Richard Aldrich. London: Routledge Falmer, 2002.

Hämmerle, Christa. ' "You Let a Weeping Woman Call You Home?" Private Correspondences During the First World War in Austria and Germany.' In *Epistolary Selves: Letters and Letter-Writers, 1600–1945,* edited by Rebecca Earle. Aldershot: Ashgate, 1999.

Hanna, Martha. 'A Republic of Letters: The Epistolary Tradition in France During World War 1.' *The American Historical Review* 108, no. 5 (2003).

Hendrick, Harry. 'Child Labour, Medical Capital and the School Medical Service, 1890–1918.' In *In the Name of the Child – Health and Welfare, 1880–1940*, edited by Roger Cooter. London: Routledge, 1992.

Johnson, Nicola. 'Penny Plain, Tuppence Coloured.' In *Patriotism: The Making and Unmaking of British National Identity, Vol 3: National Fictions*, edited by Raphael Samuel. London: Routledge, 1989.

Kramer, Alan. 'Combatants and Noncombatants: Atrocities, Massacres and War Crimes.' In *A Companion to World War 1*, edited by John Horne, 188–201: Chichester: Wiley-Blackwell, 2010.

McCulloch, Gary. 'Secondary Education.' In *A Century of Education*, edited by Richard Aldrich. London: RoutledgeFalmer, 2002.

Proctor, Tammy M. 'On My Honour – Guides and Scouts in Interwar Britain.' *Transactions of the American Philosophical Society* 92, no. 2 (2002).

Purseigle, Pierre. ' "Introduction.' In *Warfare and Belligerence – Perspectives in First World War Studies*, edited by Pierre Purseigle. Brill, 2005.

Roper, Michael. 'Maternal Relations: Moral Manliness and Emotional Survival in Letters Home During the First World War.' In *Masculinities in Politics and War – Gendering Modern History*, edited by Stefan Dudink, Karen Hagemann and John Tosh. Manchester: Manchester University Press, 2004.

Springhall, John. 'The Boy Scouts, Class and Militarism in Relation to British Youth Movements 1883–1935.' *International Review of Social History* 16, no. 2 (1971).

Springhall, John. 'Building Character in the British Boy: The Attempt to Extend Christian Manliness to Working-Class Adolescents, 1880–1914.' In *Manliness and Morality – Middle-Class Masculinity in Britain and America 1800–1940*, edited by J.A. Mangan and James Walvin. Manchester: Manchester University Press, 1987.

Steedman, Carolyn. 'Bodies, Figures and Physiology – Margaret Mcmillan and the Late Nineteenth-Century Remaking of Working-Class Childhood.' In *In the Name of the Child – Health and Welfare, 1880–1940*, edited by Roger Cooter. London: Routledge, 1992.

Tosh, John. 'Domesticity and Manliness in the Victorian Middle Class – the Family of Edward White Benson.' In *Manful Assertions – Masculinities in Britain since 1800*, edited by Michael Roper and John Tosh. London: Routledge, 1991.

Tosh, John. 'Hegemonic Masculinity and the History of Gender.' In *Masculinities in Politics and War – Gendering Modern History*, edited by Stefan Dudink, Karen Hagemann and John Tosh. Manchester: Manchester University Press, 2004.

Trumpener, Ulrich. 'The Turkish War, 1914–18.' In *A Companion to World War 1*, edited by John Horne. Wiley-Blackwell, 2010.

Voeltz, Richard A. ' "The Antidote to Khaki Fever"? – the Expansion of the British Girl Guides During the First World War.' *Journal of Contemporary History* 27, no. 4 (1992): 627–38.

Warren, Allen. 'Sir Robert Baden-Powell, the Scout Movement and Citizen Training in Great Britain, 1900–1920.' *English Historical Review* 101 (1986): 376–98.

Warren, Allen. 'Popular Manliness: Baden-Powell, Scouting and the Development of Manly Character.' In *Manliness and Morality – Middle-Class Masculinity in Britain and America 1800–1940*, edited by J.A. Mangan and James Walvin. Manchester: Manchester University Press, 1987.

Warren, Allen. ' "Mothers for the Empire"? – the Girl Guide Association in Britain, 1909–1939.' In *Making Imperial Mentalities – Socialisation and British Imperialism*, edited by J.A. Mangan. Manchester: Manchester University Press, 1990.

Published works

Poems of the Great War 1914–1918. London: Penguin, 1998.

Andrews, Lawrence. *The Education Act, 1918*. London: Routledge & Kegan Paul, 1976.

Audoin-Rouzeau, Stéphane and Annette Becker. *1914–1918: Understanding the Great War*. Translated by Catherine Temerson. London: Profile Books, 2002.

Bet-El, Ilana. *Conscripts. Forgotten Men of the Great War*. Stroud: Sutton Publishing, 2003.

Bourke, Joanna. *Dismembering the Male: Men's Bodies, Britain and the Great War*. London: Reaktion, 1996.

Bourke, Joanna. *An Intimate History of Killing – Face to Face Killing in Twentieth Century Warfare*. London: Granta Books, 1999.

Boyd, Kelly. *Manliness and the Boys' Story Paper in Britain: A Cultural History, 1855–1940*. Basingstoke: Palgrave, 2003.

Boyden, Peter. *Tommy Atkins' Letters – the History of the British Army Postal Service from 1795*. London: National Army Museum, 1990.

Bramwell, R.D. *Elementary School Work*. Durham: University of Durham, 1961.

Braybon, Gail and Penny Summerfield. *Out of the Cage: Women's Experiences in Two World Wars*. London: Pandora, 1987.

Brown, Kenneth D. *The British Toy Business – a History Since 1700*. London: Hambledon Press, 1996.

Burnett, J., ed. *Destiny Obscure – Autobiographies of Childhood, Education and Family from the 1820s to the 1920s*. London: Allen Lane, 1982.

Cadogan, Mary and Patricia Craig. *Women and Children First – the Fiction of Two World Wars*. London: Victor Gollancz, 1978.

Cunningham, Hugh. *The Children of the Poor – Representations of Childhood since the Seventeenth Century*. Oxford: Blackwell, 1991.

Cunningham, Hugh. *Children and Childhood in Western Society since 1500*. London: Longman, 1995.

Cunningham, Peter. 'Primary Education.' In *A Century of Education*, edited by Richard Aldrich. London: RoutledgeFalmer, 2002.

Curtis, S.J. *History of Education in Great Britain*. London: University Tutorial Press Ltd, 1967.

Daiken, Leslie. *Children's Toys Throughout the Ages*. London: Spring Books, 1963.

Damousi, Joy. *The Labour of Loss. Mourning, Memory and Wartime Bereavement in Australia*. Cambridge: Cambridge University Press, 1999.

Davin, Anna. *Growing up Poor – Home, School and Street in London 1870–1914*. London: Rivers Oram Press, 1996.

Dawson, Alwyn. *The Story of the 1st Chiswick – Early Years 1908–1939*, 1978.

Dawson, Graham. *Soldier Heroes – British Adventure, Empire and the Imagining of Masculinities*. London: Routledge, 1994.

DeGroot, Gerard J. *Blighty – British Society in the Era of the Great War*. London: Longman, 1996.

Dudink, Stefan, Karen Hagemann and John Tosh, eds. *Masculinities in Politics and War – Gendering Modern History*. Manchester: Manchester University Press, 2004.

Evans, Keith. *The Development and Structure of the English School System*. London: Hodder and Stoughton, 1985.

Fisher, Susan R. *Boys and Girls in No Man's Land – English-Canadian Children and the First World War*. Toronto: University of Toronto Press, 2011.

Fraser, Antonia. *A History of Toys*. London: Weidenfeld and Nicolson, 1966.

Freud, S. 'Screen Memories.' In *The Standard Edition of the Complete Works of Sigmund Freud*. London: Hogarth Press, 1962.

Fussell, P. *The Great War and Modern Memory*. Oxford: Oxford University Press, 1975.

Gordon, Peter and Denis Lawton. *Curriculum Change in the Nineteenth and Twentieth Centuries*. London: Hodder and Stoughton, 1978.

Gordon, Peter, Richard Aldrich and Dennis Dean. *Education and Policy in England in the Twentieth Century*. London: The Woburn Press, 1991.

Graves, John. *Policy and Progress in Secondary Education 1902–1942*. London: Thomas Nelson and Sons Ltd, 1943.

Grayzel, Susan. *At Home and under Fire – Air Raids and Culture in Britain from the Great War to the Blitz*. Cambridge: Cambridge University Press, 2012.

Hanna, Martha. *Your Death Would Be Mine – Paul and Marie Pireaud in the Great War*. London: Harvard University Press, 2006.

Harris, Henry. *Model Soldiers*. London: Weidenfeld and Nicolson, 1962.

Haste, Cate. *Keep the Home Fires Burning – Propaganda in the First World War*. London: Penguin, 1977.

Hendrick, Harry. *Children, Childhood and English Society 1880–1990*. Cambridge: Cambridge University Press, 1997.

Hendrick, Harry. *Child Welfare – Historical Dimensions, Contemporary Debate*. Bristol: The Policy Press, 2003.

Hopkins, Eric. *Childhood Transformed. Working-Class Children in Nineteenth-Century England*. Manchester: Manchester University Press, 1994.

Hughes, John R. *Thirty Years and More*. Derby: Derby East District Scout Council, 1996.

Johnson, Peter. *Toy Armies*. London: B.T. Batsford Ltd, 1981.

Kent, Susan Kingsley. *Making Peace – the Reconstruction of Gender in Interwar Britain*. Princeton: Princeton University Press, 1993.

Kerr, Rose and Alex Liddell. *The Story of the Girl Guides 1908–1938*. London: The Girl Guide Association, 1976.

Kramer, Rita. *Maria Montessori – a Biography*. Oxford: Basil Blackwell, 1976.

Kuhlman, Erika. *Of Little Comfort: War Widows, Fallen Soldiers, and the Remaking of the Nation after the Great War*. New York University Press, 2012.

Lawson, John and Harold Silver. *A Social History of Education in England*. London: Methuen and Co., 1973.

Lewis, Jane. *The Politics of Motherhood – Child and Maternal Welfare in England, 1900–1939*. London: Croom Helm, 1980.

MacKenzie, John. *Propaganda and Empire – the Manipulation of British Public Opinion, 1880–1960*. Manchester: Manchester University Press, 1984.

Maclure, Stuart. *A History of Education in London, 1870–1990*. London: Allen Lane, 1990.

Mangan, J.A. *Athleticism in the Victorian and Edwardian Public Schools*. Cambridge: Cambridge University Press, 1982.

Marwick, Arthur. *The Deluge – British Society and the First World War*. 2nd ed. London: MacMillan Education Ltd, 1991.

McCartney, Helen B. *Citizen Soldiers – the Liverpool Territorials in the First World War*. Cambridge: Cambridge University Press, 2005.

Mitchell, Sally. *The New Girl – Girls Culture in England 1880–1915*. New York: Columbia University Press, 1995.

Mosley, Nicholas. *Julian Grenfell – His Life and the Times of His Death 1888–1915*. London: Persephone, 1999.

Mosse, George L. *Fallen Soldiers – Reshaping the Memory of the World Wars*. Oxford: Oxford University Press, 1990.

Orwell, George. *Inside the Whale and Other Essays*. London: Penguin, 1962.

Panayi, Panikos. *The Enemy in Our Midst: Germans in Britain During the First World War*. Oxford: Berg, 1991.

Parker, P. *The Old Lie – the Great War and the Public School Ethos*. London: Constable, 1987.

Penn, Alan. *Targeting Schools – Drill, Militarism and Imperialism*. London: Woburn Press, 1999.

Pinchbeck, Ivy and Margaret Hewitt. *Children in English Society Vol Ii – from the Eighteenth Century to the Children Act 1948*. London: Routledge & Kegan Paul, 1973.

Proctor, Tammy. *Civilians in a World at War, 1914–1918*. New York University Press, 2010.

Pugh, Martin. *Women and the Women's Movement in Britain 1914–1959*. Basingstoke: Macmillan, 1992.

Rickard, John F. *Scouting around Portishead*: Published by Author, 2000.

Roper, Michael. *The Secret Battle – Emotional Survival in the Great War*. Manchester: Manchester University Press, 2009.

Roper, Michael and John Tosh, eds. *Manful Assertions – Masculinities in Britain since 1800*. London: Routledge, 1991.

Rosenthal, Michael. *The Character Factory – Baden Powell and the Origins of the Boy Scout Movement*. London: Collins, 1986.

Selleck, R.J.W. *English Primary Education and the Progressives, 1914–1918*. London: Routledge & Kegan Paul, 1972.

Sherington, Geoffrey. *English Education, Social Change and War 1911–1920*. Manchester: Manchester University Press, 1981.

Simon, Brian. *Education and the Labour Movement, 1870–1920*. London: Lawrence and Wishart, 1974.

Spalding, Alec J. *The 24th, 1908–1988 – a History of the 24th Glasgow (Bearsden) Scout Group*. Glasgow: Brown, Son & Ferguson, 1988.

Springhall, John. *Youth, Empire and Society – British Youth Movements, 1883–1940*. London: Croom Helm, 1977.

Springhall, John, Brian Fraser and Michael Hoare. *Sure and Steadfast – a History of the Boys' Brigade 1883 to 1983*. London: Collins, 1983.

Steedman, Carolyn. *Childhood, Culture and Class in Britain: Margaret Mcmillan, 1860–1931*. London: Virago, 1990.

Steedman, Carolyn. *Past Tenses – Essays on Writing, Autobiography and History*. London: Rivers Oram Press, 1992.

Steedman, Carolyn. *Strange Dislocations – Childhood and the Idea of Human Interiority, 1780–1930*. Cambridge, Massachusetts: Harvard University Press, 1995.

Steedman, Carolyn. *Dust*. Manchester: Manchester University Press, 2001.

Streatham Sea Scout Association. *Golden Jubilee of the 4th Streatham Sea Scout Group. 1913–1963*. London: Boy Scout Association, 1963.

Van Emden, Richard and Steve Humphries. *All Quiet on the Home Front – An Oral History of Life in Britain During the First World War*. London: Headline, 2003.

van der Eyken, William, ed. *Education, the Child and Society: A Documentary History*. London: Penguin, 1973.

Vincent, D. *Bread, Knowledge and Freedom: A Study of Nineteenth Century Working Class Autobiography*. London: Europa Publications Ltd, 1981.

Vincent, David. *Literacy and Popular Culture – England 1750–1914*. Cambridge: Cambridge University Press, 1989.

Walvin, James. *A Child's World – a Social History of English Childhood 1800–1914*. Harmondsworth: Penguin, 1982.

Warrack, Joan and Peggy Greening. *Girl Guides – the Edinburgh Story*. Edinburgh: County of the City of Edinburgh Girl Guides, 1977.

Wells, Edward. *Mailshot: A History of the Forces Postal Service*. London: Defence Postal and Courier Services, Royal Engineers, 1987.

Whittaker, Nicholas. *Toys Were Us – a History of Twentieth Century Toys and Toy-Making*. London: Orion, 2001.

Winnicott, D.W. *Playing and Reality*. London: Tavistock, 1971.

Winter, Jay. *The Experience of World War 1*. London: Macmillan, 1988.

Winter, Jay. *The Great War and the British People*. Basingstoke: Palgrave Macmillan, 2003.

Index

Printed and bound in the United States of America